THE JOURNEY UPHILL

Biblical Perspectives on Life, Isaiah 43 Verses 1 to 21

Stephalyn Smith

Absolute Author
Publishing House
Get published

The Journey Uphill

Copyright © 2020 by Stephalyn Smith

Publisher: Absolute Author Publishing House
Publishing Editor: Dr. Melissa Caudle
Associate Editor: Kathy Rabb Kittok
Developmental Editor: Akinlabi Ofure Odalo (Zoewriter 18)
Copy Editor: Stanley Dectiveseyes
Cover Design: Adesign

IN-DATA-PUBLICATION

The Journey Uphill/Stephalyn Smith

    p. cm.

Paperback ISBN: 978-1-64953-037-0
eBook ISBN: 978-1-64953-102-5

    1.   Religious 2. Self Help 3. Spiritual

ABOUT THE BOOK

The book, *The Journey Uphill,* carries the readers on a journey through life, giving them hope in times of adversities. It is a faith guide to empower and assure Christians to look beyond whatever uphill and challenging life experiences they might be passing through and look to God, especially in this period of Coronavirus global pandemic. The chapters are based on Isaiah 43, verses 1 to 21. This book is an excellent read to strengthen your faith in Jesus Christ as you journey uphill on the path of life.

DEDICATION

I want to dedicate this book to my family. I would like them to know that nothing is impossible with Christ. Philippians 4:13, "I can do all things through Christ which strengthen me." I am grateful for the love and support showed by you during the birthing of this book.

ACKNOWLEDGMENTS

I want first and foremost to thank the Lord, who gave me the idea for writing this book. A big thank you to my mother, my Bishop, husband, children, and friends for the wisdom and support shown during this period. And I thank the team of persons who assisted with the formation and finalization of this book.

TABLE OF CONTENTS

CHAPTER 1 1

HE KNOWS YOUR NAME 1

God is Committed to Your Total Bounce Back 3

CHAPTER 2 11

INDESTRUCTIBLE 11

Rescued from the Flames of Perception 14

There's Always an Extra Presence in the Hottest Spots
of Your Life 15

Take Your Stand 15

CHAPTER 3 16

RANSOMED 16

How Great Is God's Love? 18

You Are Chosen 20

CHAPTER 4 22

PRECIOUS 22

    He Loves You 24

    Be Patient.. 25

    Job Waited for His Change... 26

    Love Others 27

    What is the Rhythm of Your Heart? 28

CHAPTER 5... 29

I'LL SEARCH, FIND, AND RESTORE............................. 29

    Lessons from Father of the Prodigal Son..................... 31

    Paul's Plea for Onesimus: God's Letter to Parents 33

CHAPTER 6... 36

COMMANDED RELEASE 36

    Feeling Trapped?... 38

    Just for a Night 40

CHAPTER 7... 42

FOR HIS GLORY... 42

    What God Requires from His Handmade...................... 44

CHAPTER 8... 47

HIDDEN IN PLAIN SIGHT... 47

    Oasis in the Desert 50

    The Enemy's Whisper 51

    Blinded by Sin.. 52

    The Benefits of Sight and Hearing 52

CHAPTER 9 54

WHO KNOWS IT ALL? 54

    Heaven Challenges Earth 56

    Who Can See the Unknown? 57

    Unparalleled 58

CHAPTER 10 61

CHOSEN TO WITNESS 61

    YOU'VE BEEN ENLISTED 63

CHAPTER 11 68

NO OTHER SAVIOR 68

    Who's in Charge? 70

    Safe in His Arms 72

CHAPTER 12 74

YOU HAVE A TESTIMONY 74

    A Mouth That Testifies 76

    PETER'S NIGHT 77

    PAUL'S TESTIMONY 79

CHAPTER 13 80

WHO CAN REVERSE IT? 80

    Our Lord is Mighty to Save 82

    Who or What Can Stop Our Savior? 83

    Even the Rebellious Cannot Stand Against God 84

CHAPTER 14 86

FOR YOUR SAKE 86

    For Whose Sake? 87

    He Disciplines 89

CHAPTER 15 92

HOLY ONE 92

    Created for Good Works 95

CHAPTER 16 98

PATH IN THE WILDERNESS 98

    You've Got an Alternative? 100

    Be Still 102

CHAPTER 17 104

A GREATER FORCE 104

    Elisha's Army 105

    Never to Rise Again 107

CHAPTER 18 110

OUT WITH THE OLD 110

    How is Your Past? 111

    Take a Breath of Fresh Air 113

CHAPTER 19 116

OUT OF THE BOX 116

    An Eclipse of God's Power 119

    From Your Belly 120

CHAPTER 20 121

I GIVE DRINK 121

    Compelling Supplies 122

    Even the Unbelievers 124

    Look Up the Hill 125

CHAPTER 21 128

YOU'RE GOD'S PRAISE 128

    Formed for Himself 129

    Reflecting God's Praise 130

ABOUT THE AUTHOR 134

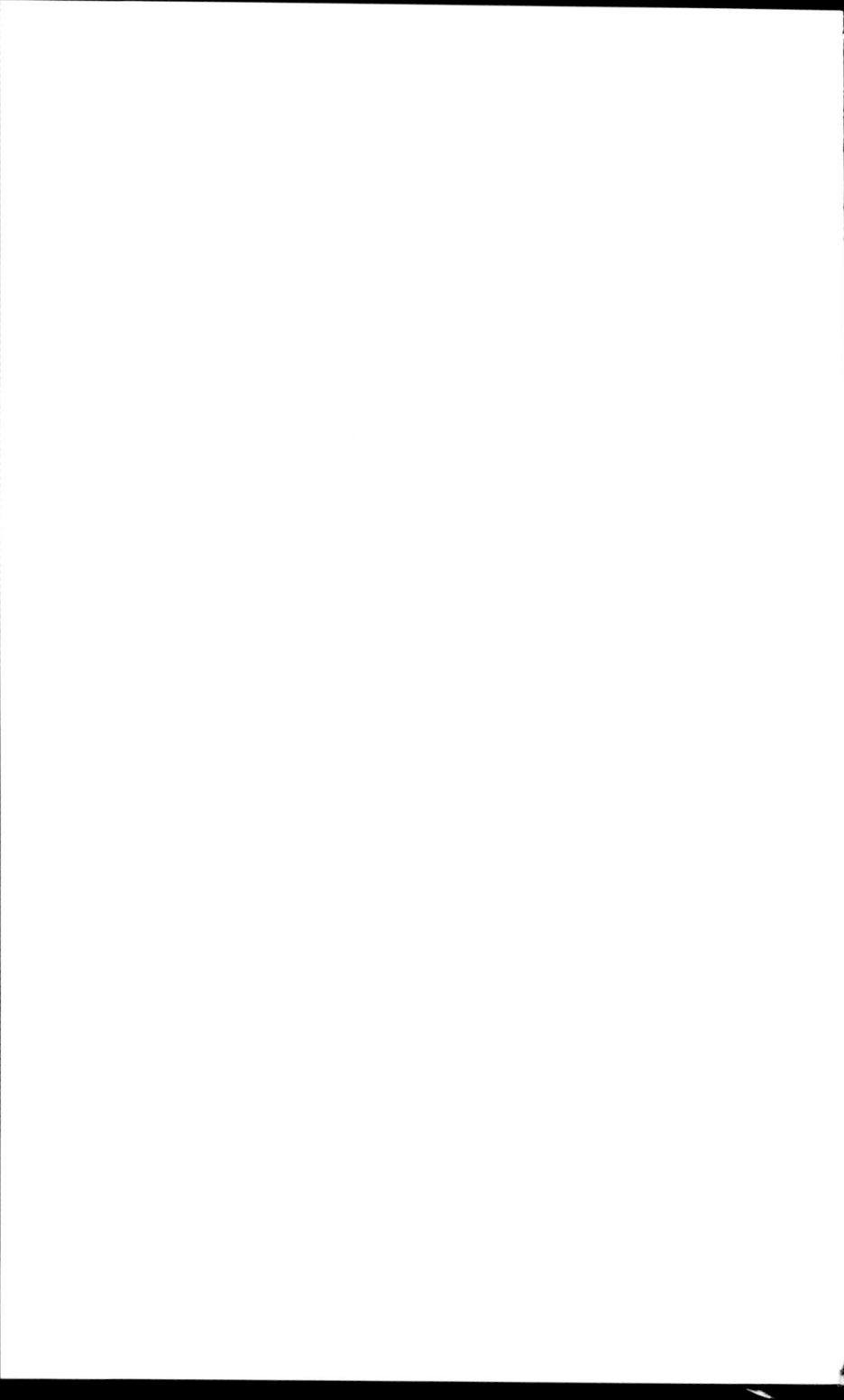

CHAPTER 1

HE KNOWS YOUR NAME

"But now, thus saith the Lord that created thee, O Jacob, and He that formed thee, O Israel, Fear not, for I have redeemed thee: I have called thee by thy name; thou art Mine." **Isaiah 43:1**

I'll like to begin this journey with you by helping you connect with a God that knows your name. How do you feel when a powerful king, noble ruler, or superior authority recognizes you? Have you ever heard someone call your name in full? How did that resonate with you?

1

One of the most common sayings of Dale Carnegie is, "Names are sweetest and most important sound in any language." It does not matter what you are called; your name is tied to your personality and sense of being.

A free online dictionary explained that *"What's in a name?"* means, *"What someone is called or labelled is arbitrary compared to their or its intrinsic qualities."* How about the connection between an individual's worth and their name?

My friend, regardless of your philosophy about names, I want you to know that God truly cares about you so much that he knows your name. I believe that's all that should matter. Isaiah 49:16 says, "Behold, I [God] have graven thee upon the palms of My hands..." What a joy and honor it is to know that our Lord and Savior, Jesus Christ, knows our name. He claims us as His own.

Regardless of who you are, what you've done, or where you're from, God cares about you. It brings great joy to be associated with a King who does not care if you are rich or poor, Black or White, educated or uneducated, fat or slim. Our Lord and Savior, Jesus Christ, does not measure us with social ideals and statuses that the world uses to categorize, esteem, or even ostracize people today.

Instead, the Lord formed us; He knew us before we were even born, and He numbered every strand of hair on our head. Now, when you think I'm talking about a God residing far and distant in the sky, you'll hardly appreciate this truth. However, imagine you could see God when He did all these things for you. What if your mom, dad, sibling, or friend told you how they were there when you were created, formed into being, and born into this world? How safe and connected will you feel when you rest within their arms? I want you to know that God is invisible, yet He is active and has never stopped being involved in your life.

God is Committed to Your Total Bounce Back

We live in an era of global losses and pain. The entire world groans in pain as their treasures get swept off by the pandemic and the socio-economic impact of prolonged lockdown. However, in the middle of these circumstances, when you begin to comprehend the depth, length, and breadth of

God's love, you will be energized to believe and receive His assuring promises.

God said, "Fear not: for I have redeemed thee," Isaiah 43:1. To be redeemed means to get back your honor, worth, or reputation. Again, I don't know your name or what it means or how it has always made you feel about yourself; but to God, your name is regal, holy, priestly, honorable, and glorious. And God is committed to redeeming your lost glory.

Regardless of how God sees you, fear is a name-changer. When you begin to indulge "feelings of distress, apprehension, or alarm caused by impending danger," you will start to lose sight of your standing in God. Fear can rename a lion to a cat, while faith can turn a sheep into a fierce bull. It's all about your knowledge of the God who is standing by your side. A sheep under a lion's protection can roar against a pack of ravenous wolves. So, why are you afraid when the Lord knows your name, and He's always at your side?

The Lord is reassuring you that fear is a waste of time because He's able and available to redeem you and restore everything you might have lost.

Interestingly, the word *'fear'* is mentioned 365 times in the Bible. We often fear the unknown, failing, the idea of starting over, or any form of change that moves us from our comfort zone. These things make our hearts beat faster. However, if we push past these sullen feelings and lies that the enemy tries to drive into our heart, to cripple our purpose, and hinder the promises that God has given us, we will realize that these feelings are just distractions from the glorious journey that the Lord has equipped us to live our lives.

As a faith-boost and assurance on your way to God's expected end, the Bible says in Psalm 27:1, "The Lord is my light and my salvation; whom shall I fear? The Lord is the strength of my life; of whom shall I be afraid?" Indeed, when you have God as your agency of rescue and deliverance, what place does fear have? And when He's your Protector and Strengthener, who can put you to flight?

Nonetheless, the Bible talks about godly fear, which is a reverence to God. Concerning this, Proverbs 1:7 says, "The fear of the Lord is the beginning of Knowledge." Also, Proverbs 14:27 says, "The fear of the Lord is a fountain of life, to depart from the snares of death." Therefore, you need to develop a godly and reverent fear of the Lord. This heart conditioning will keep you in-step with God's will and prevent you from stumbling.

Often, the tone of Scripture motivates a believer's heart to trust God, even in the darkest of moments, and hold on to the lifeline of hope, which emanates from God's love. Take a look at Romans 8:28, which reads, "And we know that all things work together for good to them that love God, to them who are the called according to His purpose." You see, your fear is weak in the face of the great truth of God's behind-the-scenes operation to make you everything you're destined to be. He has called you to a love-walk with him, and the closer you become with Jesus Christ, the less your tendency to fear.

Do you know what God is saying to you amid your valley-of-the-shadow-of-death you experienced? He says in Isaiah 41:10, "Fear thou not; for I am with thee: be not dismayed; for I am thy God. I will strengthen thee; yea, I will help thee; yea, I will uphold thee with the right hand of my righteousness." You see, the people who can make an impact and be relevant to their society, even in times of trouble, are those who trust God's presence in their lives. They believe that He is strengthening them and making them victorious in all the affairs of life.

A beautiful and intriguing story about the triumph of courage over prevalent fear features a black woman with valour. Rosa Park stood against the oppressive and racially discriminating bus segregation system in the US in the 1950s. She stood for justice, equity, and the rights of her people, probably thinking she was brave for herself, but it was for a generation to come; she was paving the way for others coming behind her.

Think about this for a moment. Do you know why you can't let fear stop you? Do you know why you have to be the brave one, even when everybody is terrified? It's because your decisions might affect a generation to come. Consequently, you must pursue what is right, despite the ever-present fear of failure.

In the Bible in 2 Timothy 1:7, it says, "For God hath not given us the spirit of fear, but of power, and of love and of a sound mind." So, where is your fear? Are you willing to find it? If you want to assess yourself, what would be the thing or things that prevent you from enjoying a sound mind?

- Is it the fear of losing your job?
- Is it the fear of being unmarried?
- Is it the fear of not having children?
- Is it the fear of not having sufficient money?
- Is it the fear of moving to a new city?
- Is it the fear of starting over?

No matter the name or label that your fear carries, our loving, caring, and powerful Lord and Savior, Jesus Christ, the Prince of Peace, is saying, "Fear not" for He is with you.

Can you imagine the assurance God is giving us? The One who controls the day and night, the universe and all creation, the One who has the whole world in His hand, has decided to keep knowing your names and dwell with you forever. This is His amazing grace!

Indeed, our journey uphill can become less laborious and threatening if we can comprehend God's unchanging love for us, which will also bring us to the place of obedience to His Words. We will navigate life as pilgrims, whose paramount desire is to please God. Hence, as we climb our mountain, navigating through life, our Redeemer is ever-present, guiding, and protecting us.

How do you replicate this love? How do you know God, who first loved you and gave Himself for you? How do you show that you believe and accept His love? Matthew 6:33 says, "Seek ye the Kingdom of God, and His righteousness and all these things shall be added unto you." This reveals that God wants us to seek His heart and not just His hand. A relationship with Jesus is vital, as the more you know Him, the greater your confidence and trust in Him become.

Here are some Scriptures that you can read in your quiet time with Jesus to reassure yourself of His continuous presence with you always.

- Revelation 21:8
- Matthew 25:25
- James 2:19
- Proverbs 23:17-18
- Proverbs 14:27
- Proverbs 19:23
- Deuteronomy 31:8
- Romans 8:28
- Psalm 23:4 1

- John 4:18
- 1 Peter 3:13-14
- Hebrews 13: 5-6
- Romans 8:15

So, what causes you fear when you know your Father, Savior, and God passionately loves you and knows your name?

CHAPTER 2

INDESTRUCTIBLE

"When thou passest through the waters, I will be with thee; and through the rivers, they shall not overflow thee: when thou walkest through the fire, thou shalt not be burned; neither shall the flame kindle upon thee." - **Isaiah 43:2**

As you journey uphill, one of your greatest fears will be the fear of being alone. Why? Because the lonely seasons of our lives can feel like the most vulnerable ones. The ultimate fear is the fear of death. However, Jesus has come to be with us through the thick and thin in our life. His presence is the confidence that takes us from one level to the other, feeling *indestructible*. However, an ardent American agnostic, Robert Green Ingersoll, argued against the possibility of 'indestructibility' of matter. He said, "If matter cannot be destroyed, cannot be annihilated, it could not have been created. The indestructible must be uncreatable."

In contrast, we believe in God, who created the elements of the earth and reigns supreme over them. He is the Creator who can kill or make us alive. He created water, fire, and air; these elements can never work against His purpose.

Isaiah 43:2 does not say believers are immune to problems, distress, pain, and discomfort. The promise that we have and can hold on to is that the Lord will be with us to put everything under the power of His sovereign will. Can you think of a situation that seemed so terrible or overwhelming that the Lord has brought you through it, glorious at that? Can you recall something that the enemy meant for evil, but the Lord turned it for your good?

Definitely, life has its difficulties—its highs and lows, but through it all, the Lord has remained faithful. There was a season in my life when everything seemed to be going wrong. I had felt defeated, yet not all was lost. It was during that time that I learned:

- Patience
- Love
- Understanding
- Reverence for Christ

Each difficulty eventually drew me closer to Christ. I learned to depend solely on God and not to lean on my understanding. I learned to acknowledge God in everything I do.

You see, the Lord cares about your every need, not just the big decisions, but the little ones, too. Today, your fire might be a court appearance; or you may feel like you're drowning in a failed marriage. You may feel the heat of the financial crisis because you recently lost your job. You may wonder why people have conspired to accuse you wrongly. You might not know how much longer you're willing to stand by and watch someone drown in their addiction to drugs or alcohol. You may feel the flames of shame, having a pregnant teenager. Whatever it is that robs you of your peace and joy, the Lord our Savior and risen King, Jesus Christ, is saying that He is with you, and these things that are meant to take you out will make you stronger. You will come out singing and rejoicing when all is said and done.

In Isaiah 61:3, "To appoint unto them that mourn in Zion, to give unto them beauty for ashes, the oil of joy for mourning, the garment of praise for the spirit of heaviness; that they might be called trees of righteousness, the planting of the LORD, that he might be glorified."

Rescued from the Flames of Perception

In Daniel Chapter 3, three Hebrew boys, Shadrach, Meshach, and Abednego, were thrown into the fire by the King of Babylon, Nebuchadnezzar, because they refused to bow to his false god. However, these boys were neither alone in that dire situation, nor alone in the fiery flames. They were preserved from harm by Jesus Christ because they fixed their mind on their Deliverer. Their faith and trust were in Christ. They were not busy complaining; they did the right thing and believed that God would rescue them.

There's Always an Extra Presence in the Hottest Spots of Your Life

God wasn't ready to secretly save men who had stood for Him openly. So, He made the King see four men walking in flames. The King declared that the fourth man was like the Son of God. Today, all we need to do is trust God. If we refuse to focus on our circumstances, then our focus must be on Christ. When we posture our response this way, we would see Him right beside us, protecting us through it all like the three Hebrew boys.

Take Your Stand

In this time of uncertainty, let us not bow to any foreign god, but let us put our trust in Jesus Christ. You see, life will throw you some curveballs, but trust that Jesus Christ will never forsake you. In Exodus 14:13, Moses told the people not to be afraid because the Egyptians they saw that day, they would never see again.

CHAPTER 3

RANSOMED

"For I am the LORD thy God, the Holy One of Israel, thy Saviour: I gave Egypt for thy ransom, Ethiopia and Seba for thee." - **Isaiah 43:3**

Have you ever thought, *Who is God*? Perhaps, you're asked to give a holistic and all-encompassing description of who God is to you. What would be your description then? What word, phrase, or sentence would you use to qualify an indescribable, unfathomable, and self-existing God? I want you to consider how amazing, awestruck, and enthralling it is to have the Creator of life and Giver of essence—an insuperable, all-powerful God—unveil and introduce Himself to you. Astounding, isn't it?

The verse that opens this chapter, Isaiah 43:3, the Lord, reminded His people of who He is to them. He reiterates that He is their God, the Holy One, and Savior. Friend, who is God to you? Do you see Him as a loving, caring, and compassionate father or a jolly friend? Or rather, do you view Him as a taskmaster, with a whip in hand, who you dread to approach.

You need to understand that your perspective of God determines your experience of Him. Imagine what Jesus' disciples thought when He suddenly asked them who they thought He was. Certainly, they knew what others thought of Him, but He wanted to know if they had the right perspective of who He was. And it was through this medium they got to know Him as Christ, the Son of the living God, by revelation.

Similarly, the verse above shows another fascinating description that God gave about Himself to His people, the Holy One. Have you ever thought about the holiness of God? The Hebrew word for holiness is 'qodes' which means to be dedicated or consecrated to God for a religious or sacred purpose.[1]

He reminded us that He is different, set apart, and sacred and that He's not ordinary. How about knowing Him as your Savior? A savior is a person who saves someone or something from danger or difficulty. On several occasions in the past, God had saved Israel from perils and protected them from other nations stronger than them. Also, His commitment to delivering them was unwavering.

Think about this. How tranquil and calm would you feel in an aircraft at about 30,000 feet when you know that there are enough life-saving gadgets to keep you safe in the event of a crash? Well, even better than that, God is with you and desires that you remain still, as you journey uphill.

How Great is God's Love?

Ransom is defined as a consideration paid for the release of someone from captivity.[2] God reiterated that He gave Egypt as ransom, Cush, and Seba in

---

[1] http://www.christianity.com.wiki

[2] https://www.merriam-webster.com/dictionary/ransom

place of Israel. God sank the mighty Egyptian army with their chariots in the red sea to deliver the Israelites from captivity. Fortunately, He is still drowning enemy armies today.

This reminds us of God's unfailing and boundless love. Indeed, He will do what is necessary to help and rescue us from danger. He promised in Jeremiah 31:3," …Yea, I have loved thee with an everlasting love…" Wow! How great and intense do you think an everlasting love would be? This is the affection that compels God to answer when you call and deliver you in times of distress.

Now, it is true that love is meaningless if it is not put into action. The good news is, God's love is not only expressed in words but also through His actions. His great love was shown when He gave His only son to endure the pain of death on a cross so that we may be redeemed.

Consequently, we are immensely comforted to know that Jesus cares for us and that He will protect us just as a mother or a father protects their child. It does not matter how significant the problem is; Jesus is the solution. Please never forget that because Jesus is the same as He was in the past, present, and will be in the future.

In truth, He does not need our help to deliver and save us; He is God. All that He requires is our praise and worship. What great joy it brings to trust in the unfailing love of Jesus. What does the Lord need but our praise and worship? Therefore, you should offer God a sacrifice of thanksgiving. Psalm 50:23 says, "Whoso offereth praise glorifieth me..."

You Are Chosen

In 1 Corinthians 1:26-31, we find, "For ye see your calling, brethren, how that not many wise men after the flesh, not many mighty, not many noble, are called: But God hath chosen the foolish things of the world to confound the wise, and God hath chosen the weak things of the world to confound the things which are mighty; And base things of the world, and things which are despised, hath God chosen, yea, and things which are not, to bring to nought things that are."

Based on the standard of the world, you may not qualify for God's love. You may not have the qualities to be approved and endorsed by God. You have your flaws and errors, yet God still chose you in place of others. Yes, the love God has bestowed on you is unconditional and qualifies you.

It is because of Him that you are in Christ Jesus, who has become for us wisdom from God - that is, our righteousness, holiness, and redemption. What is it that you were promised? Does it look too hard to accomplish? Are you saying you are too old?

I am encouraging you, as a child of God, to know that nothing is too hard for your Savior. In Isaiah 63:9, it reads, "In all their affliction He was afflicted, and the angel of His presence saved them. In His love and in his pity, He redeemed them, and He bares them and carried them all the days of old." You might be saying to yourself, it's so hard to believe these things when you are going through a difficult time, and a huge giant is standing before you. But, today, I implore you to trust God, who has a proven track record of doing the impossible.

CHAPTER 4

PRECIOUS

"Since thou wast precious in my sight, thou hast been honorable, and I have loved thee: therefore, will I give men for thee, and people for thy life." - **Isaiah 43:4**

God's love for us, as believers, brings great comfort and joy. The word 'precious' means to be of great value, not to be wasted or treated carelessly. The word honored means to be looked upon with great respect. This is how our Father in Heaven views us. If only we could see ourselves through His lens, then we would live victorious lives. We would walk and talk with authority, as we know the God we serve and assured of His magnificent plans for us.

As stated in the above verse, God reveals why He would go the extra mile to stand by the children of Israel and spot them out for honor among other nations. God referred to them with the word, *'precious.'* He called the Israelites honorable people, not because of their character, but by the favor, God bestowed on them.

The truth is, we did not earn God's affection and care through our good works or handiwork. God put His trademark of grace and honor upon us just because He chose to. Among numerous nations, God preferred and appointed the Israelites to be His people. In the same way, the Lord has ordained you an esteemed individual, without regard for what your qualifications, the amount you have in your bank account, or what any social label tag you as.

So, no matter what you have, who you are, or what you've been through in life, understand that you are precious and honorable in God's sight. That's what you have to believe about yourself because it's true. Wait a minute. Did you know that God is willing to sacrifice and give anything—gold, silver, and even people—in exchange for your life. Yes! You're worth more to Him.

However, many times, we are quick to generalize our realities. We are quick to look at the experiences of others and conclude that we are no different and no good. Therefore, we believe that we deserve no better treatment. But this should not be. Faithfully, God wants you to see yourself as precious and to experience this reality. Hear what God says in Zechariah 2:8, "...He that toucheth you toucheth the apple of His [God] eye."

He Loves You

The characteristics of God's love:

> Long Suffering
> Kindness
> Does not Envy
> Unselfish
> Not easily provoked
> Think no evil
> Rejoice not in iniquity
> Rejoice in truth

Be Patient

Human beings cannot wait patiently for God. Each day, we find ways to improve on and invent gadgets that will get things done at the snap of our fingers, such as fast-moving trains, internet connection, and fast food. We want to have our wants and needs satisfied at the snap of our fingers. Whereas this improvement has brought ease and satisfaction to our world, we often become impatient when there's a delay.

Often, when we pray to God for something, and answers to our prayers seem not forthcoming as we anticipate they would, we are quick to get discouraged. Friend, how do you respond when you're stuck in the mire of challenges? Do you ever wonder how God intends for you to respond to delays and disappointments? You have to keep your trust in God by exercising patience for your required answers. Then, remember that all things are working together for your good, even when hopes seem lost.

Recall that God prepared to bring the Israelites to the Promise Land. They waited for forty years before He delivered the promise. You have to be convinced of the truth that the waiting time is not time wasted. Beyond our knowledge, God empowers and grows us during the period, so we build the capacity to bear God's promises and judiciously use them when we receive them, eventually.

Job Waited for His Change

Job was a good and just man, yet he went through a terrible time in his life that even his wife told him to curse God and die. Job did not listen to his wife because he knew God for himself. He had a relationship with his Creator and understood the meaning of long-suffering. He knew what it was to have plenty and what it meant to have little but was still content knowing the good God he served.

You see, when you are going through your wilderness experience, you might not have any cheerleaders; it might be you and God alone. But in those down moments, will you still trust Him?

Love Others

Can you remember the last time you were kind to someone? You see, the world system is set up for us to think about ourselves and our families. But God requires us to go a little further and care for others. It's so easy to be caught up with our lives. Working long hours, drowning in bills, and the list goes on. But God requires us to care for others. Your life is precious to God, and He loves you. And He has charged you with the responsibility to extend the same love to others. Let the lives of others be precious to you also. God expects you to shine the same light on others. Value people because they are also precious in His sight.

When was the last time you checked on your neighbors to find out how they were doing? You see, you might not have millions of dollars to donate, but small acts of kindness might change someone's day. Would you be a light in this world that is full of darkness?

What is the Rhythm of Your Heart?

As believers, we must run a constant check on our hearts to ensure it is in sync with God. The Bible renounces the spirit of envy; it should not be among God's children. In Galatians 6:4, "But let every man prove his own work, and then shall he have rejoicing in himself alone, and not in another." In 1 Peter 2:1-2, "Wherefore laying aside all malice, and all guile, and hypocrisies, and envies, and all evil speakings, As newborn babes, desire the sincere milk of the word, that ye may grow thereby."

Finally, we need to examine our hearts and make it align with God's will. It is by maintaining a pure heart and connection with God that we can amply exhibit God's love. Ultimately, this will become an aroma that draws sinners unto our loving creator.

CHAPTER 5

I'LL SEARCH, FIND, AND RESTORE

"Fear not: for I am with thee: I will bring thy seed from the east and gather thee from the west." - **Isaiah 43:5**

Throughout the Scriptures, the Lord reminds His people not to be fearful, for He is with them, and He performs for them uncommon and marvelous acts. Minding the impossibilities of a situation will cause doubt if we see with our carnal eyes and not our spiritual eyes. God gathers His people from afar. He brings in the lost sheep. In Matthew 18:12-13, it reads, "How think ye? If a man has a hundred sheep, and one of them be gone astray, doth he not leave the ninety and nine, and goeth into the mountains, and seeketh that which is gone astray? And if so be that he finds it, verily I say unto you, he rejoiceth more of that sheep than of the ninety and nine which went not astray."

If you live long enough, you will eventually know how it feels to lose a loved one. Dealing with the loss of goods, time, energy, or anything else cannot be compared with the loss of a child. Can you think of the greatest source of anxiety for parents? 'Good' parents will hardly put children beneath any other thing on their priority list. From health concerns to character defects, good parents would lose sleep on the treadmill of a constant search for answers and solutions.

It doesn't matter how far and how long they've been away, don't give up. He is actively searching for them, and He'll bring them from wherever they've gone. Are you concerned about what the future holds for your children? Do you feel the life of your dear child is threatened? God is saying, "Don't worry. I am here to help you!"

Lessons from Father of the Prodigal Son

Anxiety does not solve any problem. Instead, it complicates issues. The father of the prodigal son was waiting at the door, looking out for his son. He could have waited in that uncomfortable posture forever if God didn't go to the distant land to bring the prodigal son. Imagine how much the man missed out on life while he longed for his distant son.

Trusting God to restore your child is not as easy as it sounds, yet that is the only way to allow God to do what He alone can do. He said, "I am with you…" that is, where you are at the moment, and I am going to the East and West to search, find, and restore your children. The prodigal son's father stayed back at home and trusted God to restore his son.

Contrary to the father of the prodigal son, Jacob refused to be comforted after seeing bloodstains on Joseph's coat of many colors. Interestingly, some things may appear dead, lost, and irredeemable, yet it's not the way we perceive them. Read this conversation in Genesis 37:31-36 carefully. What do you think is missing?

31 And they took Joseph's coat, and killed a kid of the goats, and dipped the coat in the blood. 32 And they sent the coat of many colors, and they brought it to their father; and said, This have we found: know now whether it be thy son's coat or no." [Did they ask about the blood?]

33 *And he knew it, and said, it is my son's coat; an evil beast hath devoured him; Joseph is without doubt rent in pieces.* [Who told Jacob that the blood was Joseph's, even though the coat was his?]

34 *And Jacob rent his clothes, and put sackcloth upon his loins, and mourned for his son many days.* 35 *And all his sons and all his daughters rose up to comfort him; but he refused to be comforted; and he said, For I will go down into the grave unto my son mourning. Thus, his father wept for him.* [We always get to choose!]

36 *And the Midianites sold him into Egypt unto Potiphar, an officer of Pharaoh's, and captain of the guard.* [Jacob never knew his son was taken away to a far country to make a place for him and his family. How

often do we also forget that our sons and daughters are not dead in any situation but just far from our reach or what we expect from them? God said, He would bring them! Do you believe God on this?]

So, what was missing? Jacob lost hope too soon, unlike the father of the prodigal son, who patiently waited till God brought his son from afar.

Paul's Plea for Onesimus: God's Letter to Parents

Sadly, not many parents understand how to receive a son or daughter when God has brought them from distant lands of sin. When your children come walking back into your life, you need to welcome and receive the one God has searched for, found, and restored. Let's see God's letter through Paul to parents.

Paul wrote:

> [8]Wherefore, though I might be much bold in Christ to enjoin thee that which is convenient,

⁹ Yet for love's sake I rather beseech thee, being such an one as Paul the aged, and now also a prisoner of Jesus Christ. [think about the basis of God's letter to you—love!]

¹⁰ I beseech thee for my son Onesimus, whom I have begotten in my bonds: [a son who needed to be restored]

¹¹ Which in time past was to thee unprofitable, but now profitable to thee and to me: [do you also have such sons—were they useless in the past?]

¹² Whom I have sent again: thou, therefore, receive him, that is, mine own bowels:

¹³ Whom I would have retained with me, that in thy stead he might have ministered unto me in the bonds of the gospel:

¹⁴ But without thy mind would I do nothing; that thy benefit should not be as it were of necessity, but willingly.

¹⁵ For perhaps he therefore departed for a season, that thou shouldest receive him for ever; [could this be your case too?]

¹⁶ Not now as a servant, but above a servant, a brother beloved, specially to me, but how much more unto thee, both in the flesh, and in the Lord?

¹⁷ If thou count me therefore a partner, receive him as myself.

¹⁸ If he hath wronged thee, or oweth thee ought, put that on mine account.

Philemon 1:8-18

CHAPTER 6

COMMANDED RELEASE

"I will say to the north, give up; and to the south, Keep not back: bring my sons from far, and my daughters from the ends of the earth." - **Isaiah 43:6**

Have you ever felt the love, calmness, security, and satisfaction that comes when your father is with you? Think about the degree of our earthly fathers' love. How far they can go to have their children safe and preserved, kept, and raised in an atmosphere of love, with full provision for living a good life.

Similarly, how far do you think our Heavenly Father would go to have you rescued from plight and pain, guilt and servitude, fear and timidity?

What's God up to with you in this chapter? God not only wants you to see that He is not just ready to search and find, find, and rescue, but also cause everything holding His children bound to release them. How would God cause this release? By the sword of His mouth -- the Word! So, God further revealed in the verse above, His desire to gather His people to Himself. Although the Scripture above refers to the universal gathering of the Jews, yet, whatever God says to one, He says to all.

Besides, God made that clear in giving us His only begotten Son, Jesus, to bring about the gathering of men unto Him. Jesus' love brings comfort to us as believers. And He resolved to be our pillar and standby. He said if He is for us, who can then be against us? The Truth is, the moment you become a believer, you become more precious than gold in the sight of God. In fact, He said you are the apple of His eyes.

Isaiah 43:6 is such a powerful verse, as it reveals the Lord's willingness to gather His scattered people, and it emphasizes the Lord's authority over everything. This Scripture also underscored that distance can never limit the most-high God in restoring and preserving His people. He speaks to the north and the earth to give up His own.

Feeling Trapped?

"Shall the prey be taken from the mighty, or the lawful captive delivered." - Isaiah 49:24

Are you under bondage at your workplace or home? Are you tired of feeling trapped? Here is good news for you. God responded to the question in the heart of the prophet in the very next verse of the Scripture above. Isaiah 49:25 says, "And I will feed them that oppress thee with their own flesh; and they shall be drunken with their own blood, as with sweet wine: and all flesh shall know that I the LORD am thy Saviour and thy Redeemer, the mighty One of Jacob." What further assurance can we have in the unchanging God, who is ready and willing to step into impossible places to command the release of His own children?

The children of Israel in verse 14 of this same chapter, said, "But Zion said, The LORD hath forsaken me, and my Lord hath forgotten me." God, in His wisdom, asked them a pressing question in verse 15, "So the LORD answers, "Can a woman forget her sucking child, that she should not have compassion on the son of her womb? yea, they may forget, yet will I not forget thee." Do not be discouraged; keep in mind that the same God of Abraham, Isaac, and Jacob, who rescued the Israelites, is still ever-present and ready to rescue you in His time.

Will He step in on time? Look at what God said in Ecclesiastes 3:11, "He hath made everything beautiful in his time: also he hath set the world in their heart, so that no man can find out the work that God maketh from the beginning to the end."

Dillon Burroughs once said, "God is never late and rarely early. He is always exactly right on time." His timing is perfect. He needs no help from us to make things happen, either in losing our chains of bondage or in fulfilling His purpose for our lives. He is God all by Himself. In His timing, as He deems it fit according to His will, He will rescue us.

Just for a Night

> "For his anger endureth but a moment; in his favor is life: weeping may endure for a night, but joy cometh in the morning." - **Psalm 30:5**

In most cases, before God steps into our situation in His time, it might seem as though the enemy is having a field day. And your night appears to be longer than necessary. For just a little while, the wicked may think they are winning the battle or have captured you, but at the appointed time, God will lay an ambush for them and set in. He will save you from the trap of the enemy, and the fowler's snare.

In Psalm 30:1, the Psalmist made a promise to God after he was lifted out of the depths of hate and oppression. He said, "I will extol thee, O LORD; for thou hast lifted me up, and hast not made my foes to rejoice over me."

After every battle won comes a victory song. Also, Psalm 121:8 says, "The LORD shall preserve thy going out and thy coming in from this time forth, and even forevermore." So, as believers, there is no reason to be fearful. Throughout the Scriptures, the Lord reminds us not to be fearful and to trust Him at all times. In Exodus 14, it says, "Moses answered the people, Do not be afraid. Stand firm, and you will see the deliverance the Lord will bring you today. The Egyptian present today, you will never see again."

Finally, in Joel 2:25-27, the Lord promises His people restoration. "And I will restore to you the years that the locust hath eaten, the cankerworm, and the caterpillar, and the palmerworm, my great army which I sent among you. And ye shall eat in plenty, and be satisfied, and praise the name of the LORD your God, that hath dealt wondrously with you: and my people shall never be ashamed. And ye shall know that I am in the midst of Israel, and that I am the LORD your God, and none else: and my people shall never be ashamed." In essence, I implore you believers to step on and believe God, your Father, for your triumph and victory song.

CHAPTER 7

FOR HIS GLORY

"Even every one that is called by my name: for I have created him for my glory, I have formed him; yea, I have made him." - **Isaiah 43:7**

"Our ultimate aim in life is not to be healthy, wealthy, prosperous, or problem-free. Our ultimate aim in life is to bring glory to God." – **Anne Graham Lotz**

Who is entitled to God's glory? Does everything in a creature reveal God's glory? What is God's eternal mandate for making and saving human beings in their fallen state?

Called by His Name

"Thy Words were found, and I did eat them; and Thy Word was unto me the joy and rejoicing of mine heart: for I am called by Thy name, O LORD God of hosts." **Jeremiah 15:16**

Formed and Made for His Glory

"What is God's glory? It is who God is. It is the essence of His nature; the weight of His importance; the radiance of His splendor; the demonstration of His power; the atmosphere of His presence." – **Rick Warren**

Glory is a state of high honor. It speaks to honor, overflow, and greatness. Whenever the living creature gives glory, honor, and thanks to God, something great happens in the supernatural. We can connect with God and be in His presence.

The Lord is worthy to receive all glory, honor, and power, for He created all things, and by His will, they existed. Jesus cannot and will not forget us unless He would neglect Himself and His glory.

Exodus 33:18, 20, says, "And he said, I beseech thee, show me thy glory [20] And he said, Thou canst not see my face: for there shall no man see me, and live."

What God Requires from His Handmade

"If you don't feel strong desires for the manifestation of the glory of God, it is not because you have drunk deeply and are satisfied. It is because you have nibbled so long at the table of the world. Your soul is stuffed with small things, and there is no room for the great." – John Piper

"Whether therefore ye eat, or drink, or whatsoever ye do, do all to the glory of God." - 1 Corinthians 10:31

- He requires our Worship
- He requires our Obedience
- He requires our trust
- He requires our faithfulness

- He requires our honesty
- He requires our commitment
- He requires us to be holy

When we assess ourselves, do we allow the world system to dictate our lives? Have we become too busy for God? We need to set apart some time to worship our Lord and Savior, Jesus Christ. We must make time for our Creator

In Matthew 5:16, it reads, "Let your light so shine before men, that they may see your good works, and glorify your Father which is in heaven." Since we are created to give glory to God, let us ask ourselves, is our light shining to draw unbelievers to Christ? Does our everyday life give glory to God, or do we put on a show on Saturday or Sunday, our designated day of worship? You see, it's in our daily interactions we should display Christ for the sole purpose of giving Him the Glory. It's not to be rich and successful; those things are secondary. So, the next time you decide to argue with a co-worker or even entertain malice, ask yourself if you are representing Christ.

Every time you decide to act on emotion or feelings, ask yourself, does this bring glory to God?

Psalm 19:1 reads, "The heavens declare the glory of God; and the firmament showeth his handiwork."

Proverbs 25:2 adds, "It is the glory of God to conceal a thing: but the honor of kings is to search out a matter."

CHAPTER 8

HIDDEN IN PLAIN SIGHT

"Bring forth the blind people that have eyes, and the deaf that has ears." - **Isaiah 43:8**

Whether it's an ornament, a precious stone, your wallet, or even your shoes, is there anything more frustrating than to be in search of something precious to you without knowing exactly where it could be found? When we find ourselves in such moments, all we do is make assumptions of where it could be and give a random search, hoping and praying that there will be a magical appearance of what we lost.

After several hours of diligent search, what happens? We may conclude that it isn't there and it's lost forever. We then give up the search and keep living with a void somewhere within. But come to think of it, what if that precious thing isn't lost? What if what you're looking for is close to you, but you couldn't see it? More so, what if the reason for your frustration is a lack of insight into God's promises for you?

Now, many believers are short-sighted and cannot glimpse into God's plans, promises, and treasures hidden for them. It remains veiled and hidden in plain sight. We scramble for things on the surface and lean on our limited physical vision to guide us through life, neglecting the place of spiritual sight and insight. No wonder the book of Isaiah 43:8 says, "...some have eyes but are blind." What a paradox!

In fact, the Bible contains lots of parables, showing the importance of spiritual sight. And to gain insight into the realities hidden in Scripture, we need the Holy Spirit. Only the Spirit of Truth can unravel the mysteries and provide insight into the unsearchable depths of God. The Scripture above speaks to a person who sees God's work but still doubts in his heart. He hears God's Word, but he's still disobedient to it.

It is to this extent that Paul prayed and said in Ephesian 1:18, "The eyes of your understanding being enlightened; that ye may know what is the hope of his calling, and what the riches of the glory of his inheritance in the saints." Coming to the knowledge of our inheritance doesn't come by physical observation and visible appearance, but by spiritual perception and enlightenment.

It is critical for us, as believers, to understand the importance of not possessing only the physical eyes and ears, but also the spiritual eyes and ears. It is through our spiritual eyes that we can see God's plans for our lives, and by our spiritual ears, we will hear His instructions and directions. How many of us received a prophecy, but it didn't come to manifestation? Frankly speaking, you'll discover that after the prophecy, your reality seems opposite to what you've received. But to be candid, it's only through your spiritual eyes that you can access, believe, and bring to manifestation what you cannot see.

Oasis in the Desert

"For I know the thoughts that I think toward you, saith the LORD, thoughts of peace, and not of evil, to give you an expected end." - **Jeremiah 29:11**

When in a desert of pain and harshness, can you believe God for a stream of blessings and joy? When the ocean of life rises heavily against you, and you have no hope of triumph, will you rest on the anchor—Jesus—that never fails? In your darkened nights, will you be courageous enough to see beyond the gloominess of the night and gain insight into what lies beneath the plain sight? Will you see into God's eternal plans for you?

In the Scripture above, Jeremiah addressed a sad, dejected, gloomy, bound, and enslaved nation of Israel. Indeed, the words God put in the mouth of His servant sounded too good to be true. Sincerely, it's hard to see the purpose in the middle of chaos or find meaning at the core of disaster. Yet, this was God's Word to His beloved children. God's Word is true and just. He can't run out of good plans for our lives -- plans to prosper us. No matter where we are in our life's journey, uphill or down in the valley, we must see the invisible if we want to gain access to God's plan and accomplish the impossible. No wonder the Bible said, "But Jesus beheld them, and said unto them, with men, this is impossible; but with God, all things are possible." Matthew 19:26

The Enemy's Whisper

> "… He was a murderer from the beginning, and abode not in the truth, because there is no truth in him. When he speaketh a lie, he speaketh of his own: for he is a liar and the father of it."
> **John 8:44**

I have discovered that beneath our unflinching affirmations are the silent whispers of the enemy. When you see possibilities, he comes with a fierce and challenging wall of impossibilities. When you take courage and step out of your comfort zone, like Peter, the enemy whispers fear into your heart. Will you damn the whispers of the enemy and reach forth in faith into God's pre-ordained future for you?

Human nature still sometimes has its way in us, despite all of God's promises. We still tend to shift ground from faith to distrust in God's promises. Many of us give up when we've barely started. We believe the lie the enemy tells us. That it will not work, it's difficult and unrealistic. He will then push us to resort to giving up. These are silent words the enemy whispers in our ears and manifest in our thoughts to derail us from God's plan for our lives.

Blinded by Sin

Finally, sin is a reproach to any man. Romans 6:22 says, "But now being made free from sin, and become servants to God, ye have your fruit unto holiness, and the end everlasting life." The understanding of the Word of God is the beginning of knowledge. Many persons are existing but are spiritually blind and deaf because they haven't had an encounter with God. You can only know God through His Word. Meditating daily on the Word of God brings you closer into His presence.

The Benefits of Sight and Hearing

- Strengthens your faith

- Understanding of the season
- A clear vision for your life
- Obedience to the Word of God

CHAPTER 9

WHO KNOWS IT ALL?

"Let all the nations be gathered together, and let the people be assembled: who among them can declare this, and show us former things? let them bring forth their witnesses, that they may be justified: or let them hear, and say, It is truth." **- Isaiah 43:9**

Imagine you have the ability to know all things, including what will happen in the future. Certainly, you will no longer be seen as human, but a god. Indeed, everyone seeks after powers or a being that is beyond them to assist in guiding them into the future and expound to them issues beyond their knowledge.

The Scripture above reveals God calling a solemn assembly of other nations to come forth and show how powerful their God is. It wasn't a contest of gods because no one can battle with the Almighty, but it was an assembly to make a public show of the folly of serving another god safe Yahweh.

Gill's Exposition of the Entire Bible expounds this verse, "Who among the idols can declare the things God has promised or shown us former things? What prophet of theirs can declare any future event, such as this, the redemption of Jews by Cyrus, foretold by the mouth of their Lord by Isaiah, so long before the accomplishment of it, or anything whatever before it comes to pass?" None could come forth.

The Bible says in Isaiah 46:10, God is the only one who can "Declare the end from the beginning, and from ancient times the things that are not yet done, saying, My counsel shall stand, and I will do all my pleasure." It goes to show the futility of serving another god. They are as limited as the people serving them. My question is, are you fully chasing after the Almighty God, the Creator of the Heavens and the Earth? Like David, is your soul waiting only on God?

Heaven Challenges Earth

A similar situation was revealed in 1 Kings 18:21-40 between Elijah and the prophets of Baal. The false worshippers were called to appear in defense of their gods. The Bible says,

> "And Elijah came unto all the people, and said, How long halt ye between two opinions? If the LORD be God, follow him: but if Baal, then follows him. And the people answered him not a word. Then Elijah said to the people, "I, even I only, remain a prophet of the LORD, but Baal's prophets are four hundred and fifty men. Let them, therefore, give us two bullocks; and let them choose one bullock for themselves, and cut it in pieces, and lay it on wood, and put no fire under and I will dress the other bullock, and lay it on wood, and put no fire under. And call ye on the name of your gods, and I will call on the name of the LORD: and the God that answereth by fire, let him be God.

And all the people answered and said, it is well spoken."

These prophets called their god all day, and not even smoke appeared on the altar. But when Elijah called on the name of his God, in verse 38, fire came down and consumed the sacrifice and the entire altar. As you journey uphill, understand that only the true God can see you through. He is the only one that can tell you the next phase of your life.

Who Can See the Unknown?

"Write the things which thou hast seen, and the things which are, and the things which shall be hereafter." **- Revelation 1:19**

You see, as a believer, you have what it takes to know what will happen in the future. How? The All-knowing God is living in you by His Spirit. Other gods cannot foresee former things, let alone the sequence of things to come. But true believers know the promises of God, His grace, His love, and His mercies. Jesus said in Matthew 13:11, "And He answered and said unto them, unto you it is given to know the mysteries of the Kingdom of Heaven, but to them, it is not given." We didn't earn the ability—we were given it. The Spirit of God can witness with your spirit concerning any issue of concern. You have access to the deep things of God. Hallelujah!

Unparalleled

> "And who, as I, shall call, and shall declare it, and set it in order for me, since I appointed the ancient people? and the things that are coming, and shall come, let them show unto them." - **Isaiah 44:7**

You see, there is no power greater than that of the true living God, Jesus Christ. The wicked refuse to hear from God. His ways are not our ways; His plans are not our plans. Just for a little, while the wicked will think that they have won. Just for a little while, they will be no more, for when the judgment of God reaches down; there shall be gnashing of teeth.

Scripture says in Psalms 14:1, "The fool hath said in his heart; there is no God. They are corrupt; they have done abominable works, there is none that doeth good."

In fact, the world is full of various religions, but one thing I know is no other god can be compared to our God, the Prince of Peace. You can search the universe, but you will never find anyone greater than Jehovah. Psalm 115:4-8, "Their idols are silver and gold, the work of men's hands. They have mouths, but they speak not: eyes have they, but they see not: They have ears, but they hear not: noses have they, but they smell not: They have hands, but they handle not: feet have they, but they walk not: neither speak they through their throat. They that make them are like unto them; so is every one that trusteth in them."

Isaiah 43:7 is reminding us that nothing can prevent God from doing what He has purposed for His people. Idols are limited in sight, and how can they stop what they can't even see coming?

So, like the children of Israel, God is saying to you today, "You shall not make for yourself a carved image or any likeness of anything that is in Heaven above, or what is in the earth beneath…" Seek to serve and honor God alone in your heart. Let your trust be absolutely on Him.

David knew better, and he said in Psalm 16:4, "Their sorrows shall be multiplied that hasten after another god: their drink offerings of blood will I not offer, nor take up their names into my lips." He said I wouldn't even put their name on my lips. Would you make the same commitment? God knows the future, and He is ready to carry you through the journey to the top. He has designed your destiny, and He hasn't given it to anyone to operate in His stead. So, stay connected. Take your mind off any distraction and let God be real in your life. Let His Word be true, and all other words be lies.

CHAPTER 10

CHOSEN TO WITNESS

"Ye are my witnesses, saith the LORD, and my servant whom I have chosen: that ye may know and believe me, and understand that I am he: before me, there was no God formed, neither shall there be after me." - **Isaiah 43:10**

Truth is light on the path of every pilgrim. As we journey in life, we'll desire and even demand trustworthiness and integrity from people and situations in our lives. Truth is the foundation of wise judgments and decisions. This is why judges declare final verdicts in the courtroom, while the human-will precedes over the courtroom of the mind. Naturally, we're always tilted in the direction of the intensity of the pieces of evidence, proofs, counsels, and testimonies, on any matter.

The court system places a high premium on the authenticity of shreds of evidence and witnesses that are presented, while the human intellect battles continually to find and uphold the truth on any matter. Deception can break any heart. Hence, witnesses are trusted with responsibility and power.

This is because every judgment, verdict, or decision will be premised on the quality of a witness' testimony. Apostle John said in John 1:1 to validate the integrity of his message to the Church. "In the beginning was the Word, and the Word was with God, and the Word was God." Apostle John stated that the message of the Gospel was verified on dimensions of every reality. The five senses are gateways to the mind, and the intensity of their exposure to any given reality becomes a seal to the authenticity of that experience.

God has a message for humanity. The truth about God and His plan for His people needs a witness, a testifier, a messenger. The Israelites are the witnesses of the Lord. He has chosen them as a family of hope and people of light to the nations in darkness. And He has always labored to let the people know and understand that He is God, the true and living God, and there is none before and after Him.

The Lord was reminding His people of the following:

- He chose them.
- No foreign god should and can take His people.
- He is the head; He sits on high.
- False gods are a reproach; they have no power; they can't foretell what to come.

YOU'VE BEEN ENLISTED

"Let a man so account of us, as of the ministers of Christ, and stewards of the mysteries of God." - **1 Corinthians 4:1**

Apostle Paul's words above is a bold statement about the content of our reputation among people. He believes that God has called every one of us to be stewards of the mysteries of God and servants of Christ. This is not just a title or position for the pulpit, but also our reputation, even in public. How do people regard you? What are you devoting your life to? Who is your master? Do you often activate your access to divine truths?

Here's an account of how Peter exemplified this Christ-centered service and Gospel-ambassadorial position.

> "Then Peter said unto them, Repent, and be baptized every one of you in the name of Jesus Christ for the remission of sins, and ye shall receive the gift of the Holy Ghost. For the promise is unto you, and to your children, and to all that are afar off, even as many as the Lord our God shall call. And with many other words did he testify and exhort, saying, Save yourselves from this untoward generation. Then they that gladly received his word were baptized: and the same day there were added unto them about three thousand souls." **Acts 2:38-41**

Every witness needs to understand the power of their words. We need to investigate the content of our conversations. What was Peter talking about? What were the mysteries that he revealed to his generation?

- **Repentance** - God wants us to bring people to a place where they can turn away from the life that has held them back in sin and kept them stuck in bondage. If repentance is not first in your message to the world, then examine the direction of your influence over the people that listens to you. False security does not eliminate danger; it only veils it from those who are heading for destruction in record speed.

- **Baptism** - The mystery of baptism is in the symbolism that the activity creates between the sinner and his savior. The water represents death and grave as the sinner is immersed in it. And at his lifting up from the water, he rises a saint who has left sin in the grave of his past, rising up to a new life of hope and holiness. What a symbolic mystery! What a blessed experience!

- **The Forgiveness of Sin** - This is the hope of every sinner. We need to get to where we're able to help men and women see a God who can respond to their repentance by offering pardon for their sins, no matter what it looks like. The love of God is our primary and central message to the world. We must be witnesses of this love before we can share it with people.

- **And the Gift of the Holy Spirit** - Our witness is not complete without the help and testimony of the Holy Spirit. He is the great guide and witness that brings Heaven to our heart and life in manifest authenticity that transcends dimensions of realities. We must tell people about God in man, who works to change us from inside out.

Finally, who will you respond to?

> The Bible says, "No man can serve two masters: for either he will hate the one and love the other; or else he will hold to the one and despise the other. Ye cannot serve God and manmon." - **Matthew 6:24**

Our love for God will pass through the crucible of service and the furnace of sacrifice. How much are we willing to give to help people find the one and only true God? How much are we available to do to ensure that someone regards us as servants and ambassadors of Christ. Are we ready to be a guide in the dark and a friend in need? You and I have been called and chosen to witness. But what kind of witness are you?

CHAPTER 11

NO OTHER SAVIOR

"I, even I, am the LORD; and beside me, there is no savior." - **Isaiah 43:11**

Relentless Search

In our world today, people search for what will save them from their quagmire. And many times, we engage in this relentless search in the wrong places. The fast pace of our contemporary society is indicative that humanity seems to be running away from something and toward whatever they believe provides freedom. There's a God-sized hole in the soul of man that demands to be filled by an all-sufficient and powerful Savior. However, this craving is often misconstrued, and people tend to settle for the next best thing.

In the Scripture above, God reminded the Israelites that He was the only source of true salvation. They were acquainted with other gods. But they discovered a vast difference between the God of their ancestors, Abraham, Isaac, and Jacob, and the pagan gods. Yahweh was the only God who related to them in terms of deliverance.

For more than four hundred years, the Israelites suffered oppression in Egypt. They had arrived in the lush green and prosperous land as the honored guests of Pharaoh but were later subjected to hard labor. Certainly, while they were in Egypt, they encountered several other gods because the Egyptians were polytheistic. However, none brought them hope or assurance of deliverance and salvation.

Indeed, it was the one true God of Israel who delivered them from their taskmasters, by a mighty hand, destroyed the Egyptian army in the Red Sea, and caused them to triumph in every battle they fought. And in the period of the judges, it was the Lord who repeatedly delivered them from their oppressors. Yet, they forget all the mighty works of God, and they sought other gods, who could neither save nor deliver. So, when God gave them His promise of rescue and restoration in Isaiah 43:11, He had to remind them that there was no other savior.

Can you relate to this? Are you seeking for salvation in an aspect of your life? Have you forgotten the God who rescued you in your darkest hour? Perhaps, you're like many people who desire the intervention of a higher power? God is reaching out to you, as the only Savior. You can end your search today by running into the arms of the God who is mighty to save.

"I am the Lord..."

Who's in Charge?

Many people end their search for the perfect salvation once they encounter imperfect saviors. But they fail to understand that all other alternatives of rescue are false. Without God, there's no true safety. Think about this. What did God mean when He said He is the only savior? It's because, as the Lord, Creator, Sovereign Ruler, and Owner of the universe, He has all authority and power over all creation. Job 9:12 says, "Behold, he taketh away, who can hinder him? who will say unto him, What doest thou?" And in John 10:29, Jesus said, "My Father, which gave them Me, is greater than all; and no man is able to pluck them out of My Father's hand."

These Scriptures reveal two reasons God is the only Savior. First, no one can be delivered from God's wrath because God is omnipotent and Lord over creation. Therefore, no man or deity can assure complete salvation. Second, God can guarantee immunity from destruction to those in His care because of His great power. God is the one in charge, and as the Lord, He's the Author and Executor of the plan to save humanity. Acts 4:12 says, "Neither is there salvation in any other: for there is none other name under Heaven given among men, whereby we must be saved." Our Father in Heaven provided us with a highway to salvation through His only begotten Son, Jesus. So, today, we can trust God for salvation by putting our trust in Jesus, who He sent to die in our place and rescue humanity from the bondage of sin and the fear of death.

Indeed, no one can save us, but Jesus Christ, no guard ring, no lodge ring, no sorcerer, no soothsayer, no man, no animal, nothing can save us but Jesus Christ. The world is full of things and people who would profess to save, but the Lord is supreme. He is the only one that can save. In this terrible Coronavirus pandemic period, only God can save us, even as we witness people die all over the world.

Are you in a dangerous situation? Is your world falling apart? Do you struggle with the oppression of sin and the bondage of fear? Is there a family crisis with nobody in sight to help? Are you in need of a savior? I know a place you can find salvation, or better, a person in whom you can find refuge.

Safe in His Arms

"Wherefore, He is able also to save them to the uttermost that come unto God by Him, seeing He ever liveth to make intercession for them." - **Hebrews 7:25**

A woman who had been living in sin for so many years was caught in adultery by several Jewish men. They had enormous rocks in their hands and were ready to stone her to death, according to what the Law of Moses prescribed for such an offender. But her accusers made a mistake. They brought her to the feet of Jesus. The Scripture above says that all who come to the Precious Son of God, He can save to the uttermost. This is what transpired in this scene that would have ended in brutal judgment. Jesus got rid of her oppressors and destroyed the sin that held her bound to her former lifestyle. He offered complete salvation, and she was safe in His arms. Likewise, Jesus, who is the same yesterday, today, and forever is willing to take you into His arms. He will save you to the uttermost and satisfy that longing in your heart. All you need to do is to come to Him today.

CHAPTER 12

YOU HAVE A TESTIMONY

"I have declared, and have saved, and I have shown when there was no strange god among you: therefore ye are my witnesses, saith the LORD, that I am God." - **Isaiah 43:12**

Except for daily sunshine, the utter darkness of the night can convince the naive that there's no hope for a brighter light than the stars and the moon. The moon and the stars that beautify the night are temporal and can only brag while the night lasts. But with the rising of the Sun, the true light, Moon, and stars will inevitably drown in the brightness of daylight. And so, the idols and gods of men fall into the sea of nothingness when God shows up in your life. In the night season, they say, "We are all you've got; pay attention to us!" But when the light of God shines into your situation, darkness and lesser lights will roll away.

So, even though it seems the devil is winning currently, yet you must know he doesn't have the final word over your life. Your testimony about God and the power of His light is enough to keep you through the darkness of the night. Know that the night is not the same as the absence of Sun; your light is waiting at the dawn of a glorious day.

You see, God always shows His uniqueness and almightiness by showing up when you're at your wits' end needing a savior. Think about when all else failed, and all you had was God. What about when at your dead end like the three Hebrew boys, and that same God showed up and rescued and preserved you? My point is, no matter how long your night season takes, you can be certain God will always show up on time. And when He shows up, you'll come out with your testimony.

However, in the face of plurality, you lose the visibility of seeing God at work in your life. When you begin to take mortal men as your God, you begin to direct divine input in your life to other gods. You also start to think it's all about what you've neglected in the place of God, who came right on time to deliver you. In the face of plurality and multifaceted decisions to make and directions to take in life, God becomes one in a million things in our hearts. And many times, what becomes gods in our hearts can be what to eat and what to wear. This little idols in our heart then blur our sight from seeing clearly the only true God.

A Mouth That Testifies

God is saying to you that after your dark moments, there's a testimony He has put in your mouth, which secures your victory. Little wonder the book of Revelation revealed that we overcome him (the dragon) by the blood of the Lamb and the words of our testimony.

When God takes you through a hard time, it's with the intent you may find a testimony to tell about His faithfulness and greatness. You must be able to decipher your results from the mighty things God has done for you and give Him all the credit for it.

The Lord is in the business of saving and preserving His people. He rescues them from impending danger because He's our Deliverer and Savior. As believers, we are His eyewitnesses to proclaim His goodness and mercy to the unbeliever. A beacon of light that shot out their darkness of skepticism and doubt. The sole duty of man is to worship the Creator, the King of kings -- Jesus Christ. Always know that God speaks to you in the night seasons of your life and there's light at the daybreak. When you were in distress, God saved you, and that makes Him worthy of your testimonies. For instance, think about the apostles and the multiple challenges they had to face as they carried out the mandate delivered to them by Jesus.

PETER'S NIGHT

Peter had his own night, but it ended in testimony in Acts 12:3-5. "And because he saw it pleased the Jews, he proceeded further to take Peter also. (Then were the days of unleavened bread.) And when he had apprehended him, he put him in prison, and delivered him to four quaternions of soldiers to keep him; intending after Easter to bring him forth to the people. Peter, therefore, was kept in prison: but prayer was made without ceasing of the church unto God for him."

PETER'S RESCUE

"And when Herod would have brought him forth, the same night Peter was sleeping between two soldiers, bound with two chains: and the keepers before the door kept the prison.

And, behold, the angel of the Lord came upon him, and a light shined in the prison: and he smote Peter on the side, and raised him up, saying, Arise up quickly. And his chains fell off from his hands.

And the angel said unto him, Gird thyself, and bind on thy sandals. And so he did. And he saith unto him, Cast thy garment about thee, and follow me.

And he went out, and followed him; and wist not that it was true which was done by the angel; but thought he saw a vision. When they were past the first and the second ward, they came unto the iron gate that leadeth unto the city; which opened to them of his own accord: and they went out, and passed on through one street; and forthwith the angel departed from him."

Act 12:6-10

PAUL'S TESTIMONY

Finally, the testimony Paul gave in 2 Corinthians 4:8-9 is not just peculiar to him, but every child. It's a testimony that also encapsulates the true response of a believer to hardship or distress. Apostle Paul said, "We are troubled on every side, yet not distressed; we are perplexed, but not in despair; Persecuted, but not forsaken; cast down, but not destroyed."

CHAPTER 13

WHO CAN REVERSE IT?

"Yea, before the day was, I am he; and there is none that can deliver out of my hand: I will work, and who shall let it?" - **Isaiah 43:13**

On a lonely, rugged, dark, and notorious alley, any face is a potential threat. Imagine you finally found yourself in the grasp of the most notorious gang, waiting for the last blow before you pass out. In that situation, anyone who dares to stand for you is a potential savior. Caught between the threat and your salvation, your life may depend on the ability of your savior. Is he big enough, strong enough, and bold enough? Does he match the danger, even if he's just a stranger? Or is he just a toothless dog, barking with its last breath, also in need of a savior?

A true savior is immune to the danger he seeks to deliver you from and into safety. Think about this; who fits into this description? Who's far above fear and has authority over death? Who has the ability to snatch the prey from the terrible and take captive the mighty? Indeed, the only true Savior is the One with limitless strength and power -- God. The One whose Words are commands and irreversible.

Isaiah 55:11 recounts, "So shall My Word be that goeth forth out of My mouth: it shall not return unto Me void, but it shall accomplish that which I please, and it shall prosper in the thing whereto I sent it." Imagine a God who can speak and enforce His Word to perform that which it was sent to do. How secure do you think you will be under His watch? He can ask your mountain to move, and nothing in creation will be able to reverse it. This Scripture also implies that if God does something in the life of His children, nothing can undo it.

Think about the Word that upholds the rising of the Sun since creation. God created the Sun and set it to rule by the day and the Moon by night. Millions of years have unfolded with multiple changes in human existence and knowledge. We have technological advancement, but the Sun and the Moon have been sustained by just the mighty decree of the irreversible God. Do you think He is weak to save you and keep you? See Hebrews 7:25, "Wherefore He is able also (think about this) to save them to the uttermost (without leaving anything out!) that come unto God by Him, seeing He ever liveth to make intercession for them."

Our Lord is Mighty to Save

The truth is, we are all journeying uphill. Our paths are not always the safest. There are threats all around, but only a few can find a savior. However, we're fortunate to have Jesus, our Savior. He's the Almighty Redeemer, Lion of the Tribe of Judah. When He stands up for us, no one can stop Him. He's a mighty Savior and Great Deliverer. No wonder the Psalmist said in Psalm 20:6 with so much assurance, "Now know I that the LORD saveth His anointed; He will hear him from His holy Heaven with the saving strength of His right hand."

Now, the first striking thing about King David's understanding of God, as His Savior, was the definiteness of the fact that He hears His people from His holy mountain. What does that imply? It implies that the limitations of the valley do not bound his Savior. He is a high and lofty one. So, His answers cannot be seasonal; it will be an ever-present help in times of need.

In fact, David emphasized how God will save His people by His saving strength! Imagine the Creator of the universe holding you by the hands during your Journey uphill. How easy and effortless will your Journey be? More so, if you decide to coast around the valley of your strength and intellectual prowess, David said, they that put their trust in chariot will only witness a great fall off the journey uphill. The Lord is the source of a believer's victory. Therefore, his trust must be in the LORD; your Savior.

Who or What Can Stop Our Savior?

The Lord is reminding His people that when He is ready to deliver them, no demon from hell can stop Him or undo it. Zephaniah 3:14-17 says, "Sing, O daughter of Zion; shout, O Israel; be glad and rejoice with all thy heart, O daughter of Jerusalem. (Why this rejoicing? Because) the

LORD hath taken away thy judgments, He hath cast out thine enemy: the king of Israel, even the LORD, is in the midst of thee: thou shalt not see evil any more. In that day it shall be said to Jerusalem, Fear thou not: and to Zion, Let not thine hands be slack. (Why? Because) the LORD thy God in the midst of thee is mighty; He will save."

You see, either God decides to bring judgment over a people or resolves to save a generation; none can alter God's will or snatch them from God's hands. "No one can deliver out of My hand or reverse My will," says the LORD. When God created the world, there was no opposition to it or any hindrances for Him. He created the world according to His will. What about when He decided to bring an end to the race of man in the days of Noah? Who could stop Him?

Even the Rebellious Cannot Stand Against God

In the book of Acts, Chapter 26, we saw the amazing story of Paul's transformation from a journey powered by darkness and wickedness against the elects of God into God's marvelous light. As rebellious as Saul (Paul) was against the true God, blinded by empty religion, the statement God made to Saul was instructive and heart-rending. "And when we were all fallen to the earth, I heard a voice speaking unto me, and saying in the Hebrew tongue, Saul, Saul, why persecutest thou Me? it is hard for thee to kick against the pricks." - Act 26:14

Indeed, it is a waste of time to fight against God's will. God told Paul; it is like kicking against the prick—you will be the one to suffer an injury on your swift Journey against the will of God. No wonder the Bible said, "The king's heart is in the hand of the LORD, as the rivers of water: He turneth it whithersoever He will." - Proverbs 21:1 God works on the unbeliever and removes blockages and difficulties according to His will.

Finally, the final words of Jesus at Calvary were, "It is finished." That implies that the work of Christ cannot be canceled or ignored. It's an eternally sealed salvation deal! God's power cannot be withheld; He always succeeds, for He has no one above Him to prevent His will from being accomplished.

CHAPTER 14

FOR YOUR SAKE

"Thus saith the LORD, your redeemer, the Holy One of Israel; For your sake I have sent to Babylon, and have brought down all their nobles, and the Chaldeans, whose cry is in the ships." - **Isaiah 43:14**

According to reputable historical accounts, Babylon was geographically positioned and particularly privileged to access great commerce and naval might. The great seas, Euphrates, was a door to the wealth of the nations, and Babylon held the master key. However, God sent Cyrus to ruin Babylon and make Euphrates less fit for navigation (by making great cataracts and raising dams in the channels of the sea).

Indeed, Babylon had enough power and wealth to make any nation shiver when they sneezed. But, when Isaiah 43 verses 14 was written, even though Israelites (the children of God) were captives of mighty Babylon and it seems no one could save them from this mighty bully, yet God prevailed over Babylon and brought it low before all nations.

For Whose Sake?

When God stepped out to bring Babylonians as fugitives, for whom was He doing that? Why will God silence such a great bully of nations? The answer is straightforward but powerful. It was an action powered by God's love for His chosen people. God is always jealous of His children. God is so jealous over His people that He will not have them serve other gods. He wants you for Himself! God said in Deuteronomy 4:23-24, "Take heed unto yourselves, lest ye forget the covenant of the LORD your God, which He made with you, and make you a graven image, or the likeness of anything, which the LORD thy God hath forbidden thee. For the

LORD thy God is a consuming fire, even a jealous God."

Hence, He's always working on their behalf. This is the reason why everyone needs to be careful when dealing with a child of God. Do you remember Jesus' question to Paul on his way to Damascus? Let's see it in Acts 9:4, "And he fell to the earth, and heard a voice saying unto him, Saul, Saul, why persecutest thou Me?" Now, who was Saul (Paul) off to Damascus to deal with? Jesus in the flesh? No! Let's see the answer in Acts 9:1-2. "And Saul, yet breathing out threatenings and slaughter against the disciples of the Lord, went unto the high priest, And desired of him letters to Damascus to the synagogues, that if he found any of this way, whether they were men or women, he might bring them bound unto Jerusalem."

We saw from this Scripture that Saul (Paul) was up against the disciples of Jesus; God's elect and chosen people. But when the Lord responded in a blinding light from Heaven, who was Paul persecuting from Heaven's perspective? JESUS! Why? God's children are hidden in Christ. To fight them is to pitch your tent against the Host of Heaven! If God could give His Son to have you, what can He not freely give you? For the sake of the Israelites, God chased out the inhabitant of the land of Canaan.

He Disciplines

Just like the foolishness of a rod, used to discipline a child (when and where that was/is acceptable), which may begin to feel advantaged or preferred above the child, so is the foolishness of an adversary when they seem to triumph over a child of God. The rod will be dumped and burned after the drill, but the child will be loved and promoted after the discipline. Think about how many times God punished His people by the hands of other nations to bring them back to their senses. Even though those nations may send sounds of triumph and joy through their land, they are absolutely ignorant that God only used them as a tool for promoting His children. I call this God's providential use of nations.

For instance, in the Book of 2 Kings 15:29; 16:7-9, we saw the story of the Assyrian army marching against the northern kingdom of Israel. Also, twelve years later, they came against the city one more time. In fact, the capital city of Samaria came under siege for three years. What was their offense all these times? In 2 Kings 18:9-12, it explains that all this was because of disobedience to the voice of God.

So, if you're currently going through the challenges of life, or someone seems to be getting away with what they've done, or they are doing to you, don't sweat over it. For your sake, Daddy will rise and fight for you. He will take on your battles and send a stern message to your adversaries. Just like He did to Babylon, He will bring your oppressors to their knees, and they will come begging at the same spot they have proudly risen against you.

This is showing us the mighty hand of God. There are no limits or extent He will not go for His people. The key is for believers to wait and trust His timing. This, sometimes, is the most challenging task as a believer. Knowing when God is at work is key to accessing peace and stability in the face of challenges. Even though God initiated their chastisement, it wasn't to send them out of Him but to bring them close. In the Scripture of 2 Peter 3:9, it says, "The Lord is not slack concerning His promise, as some men count slackness; but is longsuffering to us-ward, not willing that any should perish, but that all should come to repentance."

Finally, how do you wait for Him to act on your behalf? The answer is to stay grounded in the Word of God. Paul said in Colossians 3:16, "Let the Word of Christ dwell in you richly in all wisdom; teaching and admonishing one another in psalms and hymns and spiritual songs, singing with grace in your hearts to the Lord." And 1 Corinthian 15:58 said, "Therefore, my beloved brethren, be ye steadfast, unmoveable, always abounding in the work of the Lord, forasmuch as ye know that your labor is not in vain in the Lord." He will take down our enemies, our oppressor, for He is God, and His will is going to be accomplished. As Christians, we have to ignite our faith, kill our flesh, so God's hand can be shown in our lives. But we mess things up when we intervene. For your sake, mighty nations will fall, the things they pride themselves in will be no more.

CHAPTER 15

HOLY ONE

"I am the LORD, your Holy One, the creator of Israel, your King." - **Isaiah 43:15**

On the one hand, the pandemic has brought significant loss and grief, but on the other hand, there are blessings in disguise. I'm not trying to be insensitive. I only want you to read the signs on the flip side of the cold coin. You see, aside from deaths, we've gained more value for life. Even with issues about face masks and ventilators, we've gained more value for fresh air and working lungs.

And aside from the economic loss, we have gained more value for rest, peace, and contentment. Romans 8:28 says, "And we know that all things work together for good to them that love God, to them who are the called according to His purpose." Despite the frustration caused by the lockdown, such as social distancing, we've been made to appreciate the hugs and the love that family and friendship brings. And aside from the virus, we have gained value for health workers and hand sanitizers.

You wonder where I'm going with this. Here is my point. Our generation is not the first to go through crises and challenging times. Israel also went through difficult times on their way to the promised land; however, the good news was that God was with them all the way. They faced challenges, yet with an assurance of divine presence and rescue.

Isaiah 43:15 is simply the description of the personality of God to His people. Usually, no one can describe a person more than him, so God is best to explain Himself to His people. The previous verses reveal the promises and assurances; now, it's time to reveal the personality of their God.

Stephalyn Smith

Have you ever developed a strong confidence in the words of a man, that you were so sure he will never fail you? What gave you such assurance? For most people, it's because of the integrity of the person. Here, God presents Himself to Israel as holy. Holiness is not a title for God but His personality, His nature, and the quality of His attribute. The root word for holy is *qadosh* (Hebrew) and *hagios* (Greek), and it means "set apart, sacred, and sanctified."

No other creature shares a similar description of holiness with God. He is holy in all His ways; His love is holy; His mercy and justice are holy. Holiness is a symbol of His purity and perfection. He is the standard of purity, and nothing can be compared to that nature.

As believers, we are called to be holy. All through the journey of the Israelites, God kept emphasizing to them to separate themselves from all unclean things and be holy as God is holy. They are His people, and He has set them apart for His glory. Different from other people on earth. They are holy unto God not because of what they have done but because of who God is – a holy God.

You see, the ultimate goal as believers is to see God and be like Him -- holy as He is holy. The Scripture says in 1John 3:2, "Beloved, now are we the sons of God, and it doth not yet appear what we shall be: but we know that, when He shall appear, we shall be like Him; for we shall see Him as He is." Being holy like our God should be our priority as we journey uphill.

This goal seems impossible with the human flesh, but with the help of the Holy Spirit, we can attain a life of purity and sanctification, free of sin and double standard, like God.

Created for Good Works

God also presents Himself as their Creator. The context of this is not referring to the universal creation of all other animals and creatures; neither does it refer to the creation of unbelievers, but they are created unto God in purity and sanctification. Apostle Paul said in Ephesians 2:10, "For we are His workmanship, created in Christ Jesus unto good works, which God hath before ordained that we should walk in them." That is, God created and ordained you for good works. The aim is to partner with God on earth as His stewards, serving His interest everywhere through your lifestyle and deeds.

He created you as light and placed you in this dark world to shine and dispel the darkness. And when men see your good works, which reflects the pure light of God's holy nature inside you, they will glorify the Father in Heaven. So, abide in the purpose for which you were created. It's not for yourself, and what more, just like a Moon positions itself near the Sun to reflect the light on the Earth, you also abide in the circumference of God's marvelous light so that you can reflect His glory and power.

Kingdom Lifestyle

Moreover, God spoke boldly of Himself as their King. This might indeed be thought to be absurd; because back then, there was no semblance of a kingdom setting among them. They were like men wandering from place to place and fighting battles with other kings.

Usually, when there is a war between nations, the strategy and plan are executed in the palace, and mostly the King leads the people to battle. But what is the hope of a nation without a king? Well, God calmed them by introducing Himself as their King.

And when God is for you, all those against you will fall like packs of cards.

God was their King, and He will serve their interest always. Babylon may have taken them captive, but their King was coming for them. God being their King, reflects hope, victory, and restoration. However, there is a need to acknowledge God as their King. And every King has a kingdom with principles governing the kingdom.

Like the Israelites, God is calling you to a Kingdom lifestyle. He wants to be your God and also your King. A good king serves the people and always desires to see them prosper. But you have to abide by the lifestyle of this kingdom. Accepting God as your King is subjecting yourself to the principles of His Kingdom. That was why Jesus came, to present the Kingdom of God to us on earth. The Word of God is filled with Kingdom principles and values. One principle among them is love. Walk and live in love and peace with all men. Paul said, in Romans 14:17, the Kingdom of God is in "...righteousness, and peace, and joy in the Holy Ghost."

So, seek God's help through the Holy Ghost to live Holy in this kingdom and live in peace with all men.

CHAPTER 16

PATH IN THE WILDERNESS

"Thus saith the LORD, which maketh a way in the sea, and a path in the mighty waters." - **Isaiah 43:16**

Jesus never promised us a ride free of challenges through life; neither did He give His Word that believers will never face situations that make it look as though God is silent and far away. As believers, we are not immune to problems, but rest assured that the Lord will deliver us according to His will.

Psalm 46:1 says, "God is our refuge and strength, a very present help in trouble." You know, I have come to realize that whenever we find ourselves in situations stuck between a rock and a hard place, it's an opportunity to experience the almightiness of God. Think about the Scripture above carefully. Do you discover something there? I mean, how can you have an experiential knowledge of God as an ever-present help in times of trouble if you've never been in trouble?

Now, don't misunderstand me. I'm not saying you should be in trouble to know God. What I'm driving home here is that during our times of trouble, as children of God, they are not meant to break us, but unveil to us a supernatural dimension of Papa -- God. God's more exalted when all else fails, and He steps right in and works things out for you.

So many times, we face situations that seem very heavy for us as humans to carry, even sometimes allow us to question our faith and repeatedly ask if God is still alive or even concerned about us. When this happens, there is a phrase that can help in Philippians 4:6, "Be careful for nothing; but in everything by prayer and supplication with thanksgiving let your requests be made known unto God." In this, we can draw our strength, knowing that when we, prayerfully and with a thankful heart, go to God, knowing indeed that when we pray in the name of Jesus, it is signed, sealed, and delivered.

You've Got an Alternative?

Friend, I have some questions for you! Is God your last resort or one of the means to your ambitious end? When the seas of life become troubled by the storm of fear and uncertainty, is God your only answer or one of several options?

The truth is when in need, pain, or distress, we often forget that the Lord's promises are ever-present, and God will help us come through. Our momentary afflictions may knock us off guard and make us anxious. But think about David in the book of Psalm 63:1-2. David found himself in a dry and thirsty land; what do you think David should have been occupied with? Planning how to dig water wells, right?

But it was amazing to discover that David turned from his situation to God. Glory to God! Instead of first engaging his limited mind on how water will burst forth in a wilderness, David cried and said, "O God, thou art my God; early will I seek thee: my soul thirsteth for thee, my flesh longeth for thee in a dry and thirsty land, where no water is; To see thy power and thy glory, so as I have seen thee in the sanctuary." Wow! What a man David was. He understood that the most significant asset he had to bring a solution to an earthly predicament or problem was THE LORD.

David was so sure that the answer to his cry was not mere water, but the Lord—the Maker of all things. He must have said, "I know if God is with me, water can even come out of the rock as He did for the Israelites."

The same thing applies to you, my friend! Why not take your eyes off your problems and see the living God stepping into it with healing in His wings? When we come to the understanding of the Lordship of Christ, our hope will rest on Him. And because He loves you, you can walk through the fire, rest assured that He would be there with you. Never allow the dryness and shallowness around you to breed the thoughts of seeking alternatives to God on your Journey uphill. Set your heart on the

Lord like David and see how He will show up and break your fallow grounds and do the impossible in your life.

Be Still

"Be still and know that I am God: I will be exalted among the heathen; I will be exalted in the earth." - **Psalm 46:10**

For the Lord to operate on our behalf, we have to let go of what we know or think we know and allow His perfect will to work through us. It is not easy when your manager has done some injustice to you, and your flesh is twitching to give him or her a piece of your mind. That is your will, but if you allow God's will to prevail, then He will deliver you from all injustice and all hurt. Believe me; there is a great reward in God for obedience.

The Word says obedience is better than sacrifice. It is better to obey and conform to the will of God right from the beginning than to disobey and start looking for solutions to situations that were caused by disobedience. When we do our part of obeying the dictates of the Word, it makes it very easy to claim the promises in the Word of God when things seem very tough and challenging.

One such promise is found in the book of Jeremiah 29:11, "For I know the thoughts that I think toward you, saith the Lord, thoughts of peace, and not of evil, to give you an expected end." This passage comes with the assurance of safety in Christ. However, there is no promise of ease. Looking at the preceding passage, we would see the suffering the children of Israel underwent in exile. Still, even in all their trials and tribulations, this was the promise God gave to them, which is also the promise we should firmly hold onto as Christians in this world today.

Finally, what needs to be done is for you to fully hand everything to the One in control of times and seasons and watch Him perform wonders in that situation you think is out of your control. He alone is in control and has planned your life according to His will.

Be still, feed on the Word, communicate to the Father in prayers, obey the statutes of God, and watch how God will work miracles in your life.

CHAPTER 17

A GREATER FORCE

"Which bringeth forth the chariot and horse, the army and the power; they shall lie down together, they shall not rise: they are extinct, they are quenched as tow." - **Isaiah 43:17**

It has become a cliché among Christian folks to say, "The battle is the Lord's." Do many people really believe this true assertion? I guess not! The reason is that after making our bold proclamation or declaration of faith, we still walk through life trying to fix things by our strength and intellect. We seem not yet rest assured that when you allow the Lord to fight, the battle is won. God has never lost a fight, and He won't start now. He is the Lord Almighty. It doesn't matter if an army surrounds you; the Lord will protect you.

There is a spiritual covering that comes with your new birth experience. The moment you surrender your life to Christ and live according to His Holy Word, the Lord automatically shall cause your enemies to be crushed and never to rise again. The great force of the Lord's army will extinguish and snuff out the enemies, and you shall have your peace.

Elisha's Army

Elisha, as a man of God, understood and easily identified the Lord's army as the greater force. The Bible encourages us to "look not at the things which are seen, but at the things which are not seen," in II Corinthian 4:18. That is just what Elisha did in II Kings 6:12-17. The Kingdom of Israel is at war with the Kingdom of Aram, but the King of Israel seems to predict Aram's every move. Everywhere Aram's army goes, Israel is one step ahead – so much that the King of Aram assumes that there was a spy in his camp. But there is no spy; rather, God is speaking to the prophet and giving him inside information – divine knowledge and divine vision – and Elisha passed that knowledge on to the King of Israel.

When the King of Aram realizes what happened, he sent his army to find Elisha and capture him. So, one morning, Elisha's servant pulled back the curtains and discovered that Aram's army totally surrounded their house. Just as many of us would do in his situation, he called out in fear and panic, "And when the servant of the man of God was risen early, and gone forth, behold, an host compassed the city both with horses and chariots. And his servant said unto him, Alas, my master! how shall we do?" (vs.15.) Now, we might expect Elisha to come up with a cunning plan to make an undercover exit or to hide somewhere, hoping they won't be found, or to hand himself over to make things go as smoothly as possible. Instead, Elisha calmly replied, "And he answered, Fear not: for they that be with us are more than they that be with them." (vs.16). Elisha's servant was completely perplexed, so Elisha prayed, ".....O LORD, open his eyes, that he may see!" (vs.17).

We can see from the little background given that there is in existence, a greater force that is always on the alert to fight for God's people. Many times, believers look at the physical and become confounded. If only our spiritual eyes can be opened to see that the army of God is ready to smite our enemies who, in the form of issues and challenges of life, surround us, we will rest from all panic and take a more consistent ride up the hill. We see the hopelessness of our situations when we look only at the physical. However, they that are with us are more than be with them because "Ye are of God, little children, and have overcome them: because greater is he that is in you, than he that is in the world." (1 John 4:4). We need not fear anymore!

Never to Rise Again

Anyone standing between God and His people is ready to be crushed and never to rise again. The story of the children of Israel and the crossing of the Red Sea is quite a familiar one. The enemy came against the people of God in Exodus 14:6-9, like a flood. It appears that the end is near, with the Red Sea in front of them and the Egyptian army fast approaching from the rear. At the last moment, God showed up and rescued His own. What is more, the Egyptian army perished in the Red Sea, and they were never to rise again.

What was God's plan? Remember, God was the one who hardened Pharaoh's heart to pursue them. Why? To grant His people a complete victory and have the Egyptians never to rise again. The wicked are blinded by their anger. The folly of Pharaoh and his army were exposed as they unwisely pursued God's people. As a believer, what do you do with your fear? What is your response to the growing pandemic of fear plaguing the world around you? Fear not! Call on the greater force, and they are ever ready to swing into action, for the battle is not yours but the Lord's.

Think about the redemption plan, too, how God perfected our deliverance from sin, poverty, diseases, pain, and all the outcome of the fall. We were once alienated from the commonwealth of Israel, but the Lord brought us into rest by the finished work of Christ. The Egyptians were under servitude the same way an unbeliever is under servitude under the devil—a wicked taskmaster. God is bringing to light in that Isaiah 43:17, His plan not just to save, but to completely save us from our troubles and predicaments.

We need not over flog the issue that the battle is for the Lord and not our business. Have you wasted all your strength worrying when you could have been worshipping God for your victory? Come on now! The battle is not yours; give it back. Quit trying to do God's job for Him; He wants to fight for you! The best we could be is to be God's battle-ax. Our choice is now to become a potent weapon of war or not. But the crux of the matter remains that "because of God's greater force, you need not fear, for the battle is already won."

CHAPTER 18

OUT WITH THE OLD

"Remember ye not the former things, neither consider the things of old." **- Isaiah 43:18**

No one attempts to move forward, gazing backward. The past represents our history - what was done and dusted. The truth is, we all have some good memories in our past that we wish could remain with us, and likewise, the children of Israel. They were in captivity, and God told them, through the prophet, not to remember the past.

That may sound awkward to them because, as at then, their past was, in fact, much better. They had great memories of how God saved them from Egypt and parted the red sea for them to go through; how God conquered nations that were obviously mightier than them and gave them landslide victory; how they ate in the wilderness for forty years directly from heaven's kitchen; how they eventually inhabited Canaan - a land flowing with milk and honey. Yet, God was saying to them, remember not the former things. Why? Let's find out

How is Your Past?

Is your past fascinating like that of the Israelites, or is it the exact opposite? Perhaps nothing is interesting about your past; neither is there much to write home about. Is your past as horrible as that of Rahab? And you think it's not possible ever to make amends, or you had your share of struggles full of pain. Did you also make mistakes that seem unforgivable? Like David, have you made mistakes and have the scars to show?

What about Paul, a man who persecuted the Church and killed several Christians? I can only imagine how sorrowful he was when he saw the children or surviving families of the people he killed. I mean, days when the thought of his past made him shed tears. Do you share a similar experience? God is saying to you, remember not the past, let go of the disappointment from your close friend, let go of the failures, the targets that you couldn't meet up with, the good deeds you wish you did, let it go completely. Remember not the former things because, according to God, they are old stuff.

Apostle Paul also shared this secrete as his way of life. In Philippians 3:13, he said, "Brethren, I count not myself to have apprehended: but this one thing I do, forgetting those things which are behind…" If there was anyone that had a past, fierce enough to hunt the present, it was Paul. Yet, he said, there is one thing he does not once and for all, but once and again. He makes it a personal responsibility to switch his mind away from his past. He knew if he must advance, there is the need to forget the past.

Even if they were amusing, let go of them, because hanging on to the past draws you away from the future. Let it go. You see, the past is like a mirage, you can only see it, but you can't handle it. There is nothing you can do about the past, just as it's a dysfunction for a time to tick backward. So, let it go.

Great men today also had many things to let go of in their past.

Take a Breath of Fresh Air

Now, take a deep breath and see into the future God has for you. Any lasting relationship is built on the principle of regularly forgetting what happened in the past. God said, even your iniquities, I will remember no more. So, take a fresh breath of hope and joy.

God commanded the children not to remember the good old days because He has greater things ahead for them. They have seen some great works of God, but they are about to see the greater works of God.

Apostle Paul said in Philippians 3:13-14, "…forgetting those things which are behind…" He has learned to switch his mind from the past into the future. He wasn't going to allow his past to hinder him from the great things God has for the future. He wasn't going to drop his head like a fruit hanging on a tree; rather, he will raise it high like the morning Sun.

Friend, there are great things ahead of you. Every one that emerged great today had some horrible past that could have held them stuck. But they chose to let the past go and face the future. You may have heard about Bill Gates, who was once the richest man in the world. But do you also know that his company, Microsoft, was not his first attempt at success? Yes, it wasn't.

Bill's first company, Traf-O-Data (a device that could read traffic tapes and process the data), failed miserably. Then Gates and his partner, Paul Allen, tried to sell it, and even then, the product wouldn't work. At that point, they seriously contemplated admitting failure. All the sleepless nights and struggles seemed futile and useless. But amid this obvious obstacle to success and wealth, they tried again. Gates and Allen didn't let the failure of Traf-O-Data stop them. Hear how Allen explained the impact of that failure, he said, "Even though Traf-O-Data wasn't a roaring success, it was seminal in preparing us to make Microsoft's first product a couple of years later."

Well, they could have held on to their failure and settle for misery, but they chose to shake off the dust, and what was the outcome? Microsoft emerged. You see, there are great things ahead of you -- great testimonies, inventions, and remarkable ideas. But as you journey uphill, make up your mind to travel like Paul, who said, forgetting the things which are behind.

Letting go is the first step to facing the future. The journey ahead is not a slope downhill; it's a journey uphill, and trust me, the greatest risk is to get stuck with the past. So, what do you do? Learn from the past, thank God for the good things that worked, and once in progress, step into each day full of hope and high expectation.

CHAPTER 19

OUT OF THE BOX

"Behold, I will do a new thing; now it shall spring forth; shall ye not know it? I will even make a way in the wilderness, and rivers in the desert." **– Isaiah 43:19**

Have you ever tried to collect an item such as a toy from a little child, and he refused to release it? For most adults, they simply present a better toy. And without further hesitation, the child will let go of the old toy and stretch his hand as far as he can to receive the new one. In the previous verse, God told the children of Israel to forget the past because He was set to do something new. You see, God was telling them that the future is great and wonderful than what He has done in the past.

"The plans I have for you are good," says God. He will feed His people in lack; He will make a way, even when it seems impossible with our carnal eyes. What they have seen was great, but the greater is about to happen -- amazing testimonies beyond the ordinary. So, God is saying, trust Me.

Springing Forth

> "…now, it shall spring forth."

That Scripture paints a beautiful image of the silent but certain gradual growth of events in God's providence. See Mark 4:26-28, "And He said, so is the Kingdom of God, as if a man should cast seed into the ground; And should sleep, and rise night and day, and the seed should spring and grow up, he knoweth not how. For the earth bringeth forth fruit of herself; first the blade, then the ear, after that, the full corn in the ear. But when the fruit is brought forth, immediately he putteth in they shall spring forth as it were in a day. Did you observe what Jesus said in the parable? He said the farmer does not know how the seed grows into the harvest. Awesome!

You see, you may not be able to explain the great happenings of God in your life, but it will be undeniable. You remember when the Kings were going to war in 2 Kings Chapter 3, and suddenly they needed water, and there was none. Then they called for Elisha, and he prophesied in verse 17, "For thus saith the LORD, Ye shall not see wind, neither shall ye see rain; yet that valley shall be filled with water, that ye may drink, both ye, and your cattle, and your beasts." So, expect a spring forth of great things from now. Expect a supernatural new-normal in your life.

Just like a germinating herb, God said the good intention and plans He has for you will spring forth. Think about the silence, unnoticed, and despised days seeds spend in the ground. You may think it will never spring forth again, but alas! It burst forth in newness and life. God said the same thing would happen to His children. Even though it may seem your breakthrough is delayed, God said the way it will come forth; nothing will be able to hinder it.

An Eclipse of God's Power

"…I will even make a way in the wilderness."

Napoleon Bonaparte once said, "Impossible is the word found only in a fool's dictionary." And our God is the only wise God. He said in Jeremiah 32:27, "Behold, I am the LORD, the God of all flesh: is there anything too hard for Me?" The answer is an affirmative no.

Just as Israel in the wilderness, between the Red Sea and Canaan, was guided and supplied with water by God, there will be a new dimension of deliverance with manifestations of God's power and love eclipsing the old. God makes a way in impossible places. What is that situation that seems impossible for you? Have you sent in an application, and it was refused, or you have attempted some opportunities, but was told you didn't measure up?

Here is the good news. God is lifting the gates already. He created dry land through a sea for the Israelites to walk through; He will make way for you. In Isaiah 41:17-19, the Bible said, "When the poor and needy seek water, and there is none, and their tongue faileth for thirst, I the LORD will hear them, I the God of Israel will not forsake them. I will open rivers in high places, and fountains in the midst of the valleys: I will make the wilderness a pool of water, and the dry land springs of water. I will plant in the wilderness the cedar, the shittah tree, and the myrtle, and the oil tree; I will set in the desert the fir tree, and the pine, and the box tree together."

From Your Belly

"Rivers" express the influences of the Holy Spirit, according to John 7:37-39. However, Israel's literal restoration is included in that verse. In Isaiah 11:15-16, "And the LORD shall utterly destroy the tongue of the Egyptian sea; and with his mighty wind shall he shake his hand over the river, and shall smite it in the seven streams, and make men go over dryshod. And there shall be a highway for the remnant of His people, which shall be left, from Assyria; like as it was to Israel in the day that He came up out of the land of Egypt."

God brought out water from the rock when His people were thirsty, so expect a similar provision from God. So, no more dryness in your life because God is set to generate water where everyone least expects. Therefore, open up your mind and receive the refreshing of God's mercy and grace.

CHAPTER 20

I GIVE DRINK

"The beast of the field shall honor me, the dragons and the owls: because I give waters in the wilderness, and rivers in the desert, to give drink to my people, my chosen." - **Isaiah 43:20**

There is an undeniable hierarchy in nature, and humans are definitely more advanced than all of God's creation. Man is ranked higher than other animals because of our mind and ability to form societies. But one thing that unites creation is our dependence on our source -- God. The birds of the air, cattle of the field, fishes in the sea and all manner of plants depend on God to satisfy their needs, and so does man. This makes creation to gravitate toward the all-sufficient provider, who can give waters in the wilderness and rivers in the desert.

Throughout the Bible, God wrought mighty wonders to bless and cater for His chosen nation, Israel, and this made His name great before other nations. Well, God is still doing the same today!

Compelling Supplies

In the Scripture above, there's a resultant effect of the blessings of God over His people. It's a full encapsulation of what happens when God does an unprecedented miracle for His people in impossible places. It announces the glory of our God among the earthen when God does the unimaginable. I mean, in our previous chapters, we saw how God committed Himself to do something no man can gainsay or claim as accomplished by his power.

In fact, He challenged other gods to show there might and foresight if it will match His matchless nature. Do you know that in all these verses, God never disclosed how He would bring water into the wilderness? Have you ever imagined how that can be possible? Indeed, naturally, to have water in the wilderness requires countless days of and intense technological input. But here is God in His infinite power, saying, "I will do this without your input!"

A wilderness is described as a place that is uninhabited or inhabited only by wild animals. Now, God is saying that even the places inhabited by the beast of the field and wild animals, He will make water available for them. How does that sound? God cares about the animals in the wilderness, and He can't stand and watch them die of thirst, how much more you, His beloved.

Jesus also made a similar statement in Matthew 6:26; He said, "Behold the fowls of the air: for they sow not, neither do they reap, nor gather into barns; yet your Heavenly Father feedeth them. Are ye not much better than they?"

Here is my answer; you are better than all animals because you are created in the image and likeness of God. So, let go of the thought that reminds you of your sins and weaknesses, quit drawing away from God, thinking you are not worthy. If He provided water in the wilderness, then He can make provisions for you also.

Even the Unbelievers

More so, the beasts, dragons, and the owls are image or symbols of idolaters, defiled with blood and pollutions, dwelling like dragons, etc., in the wastes of Gentile ignorance: even they shall be converted.

Think about Psalm 148:7-13, "Praise the LORD from the earth, ye dragons, and all deeps: Fire, and hail; snow, and vapor; stormy wind fulfilling His Word: Mountains, and all hills; fruitful trees, and all cedars: Beasts, and all cattle; creeping things, and flying fowl: Kings of the earth, and all people; princes, and all judges of the earth: Both young men, and maidens; old men, and children: Let them praise the name of the LORD: for His name alone is excellent; His glory is above the earth and Heaven."

All living things must honor our creator, Jesus Christ, as He provides for His chosen people. Just as our natural father loves and cares for us, so do our spiritual Father, Jesus Christ provides for us in times of need.

Look Up the Hill

Check out this assurance by King David.

> "I will lift up mine eyes unto the hills, from whence cometh my help.
>
> My help cometh from the LORD, which made Heaven and earth.
>
> He will not suffer thy foot to be moved: He that keepeth thee will not slumber.
>
> Behold, He that keepeth Israel shall neither slumber nor sleep.
>
> The LORD is thy keeper: the LORD is thy shade upon thy right hand.
>
> The sun shall not smite thee by day, nor the moon by night.
>
> The LORD shall preserve thee from all evil: He shall preserve thy soul.

The LORD shall preserve thy going out and thy coming in from this time forth, and even for ever more."

Psalm 121:1-8

This was a Psalm of David. Quit looking up to man for help, look but to God. No matter what the situation may be, keep your eyes fixed on Him. A songwriter says, "All of my help comes from the Lord." The Bible is filled with the diverse assurance of God's goodness and readiness to save and provide for His own.

God provides for the beast and also His chosen one. Are you God's chosen? He chose you out of every nation and people and separated you to Himself. So, look up to God alone. The medical report may not look good, your child may be suffering from addiction, the bills may have piled up, and the debts may look as though your entire life savings will not be sufficient to clear it. Just look up to God. Help wasn't coming forth from anywhere for the Israelites because they were held captive in Babylon -- the world power in their days. But they looked up to the Hill, the only place they could receive help.

Too often, we tend to calculate that God will help us; we try to take steps of faith, but they are smart steps. We look up to our church members and siblings and deceive ourselves into thinking we are looking up to God when, in the real sense, we are expecting humans to come through for us.

Remember how God used the ravens to feed Elijah when there was a famine in the whole land. Who could have expected such a divine interference? In 1 Kings 17:2-4, it says, "And the Word of the LORD came unto him, saying, get thee hence, and turn thee eastward, and hide thyself by the brook Cherith, that is before Jordan. And it shall be, that thou shalt drink of the brook; and I have commanded the ravens to feed thee there."

So, don't be downcast, God is near, and you are in your season of abundance and the best of your days. God is making provisions from extraordinary sources and impossible places. Hold on tight, the dry seasons are over, the deep is about to burst forth into abundance for you, and you will be satisfied.

CHAPTER 21

YOU'RE GOD'S PRAISE

"The people have I formed for myself; they shall show forth my praise." - **Isaiah 43:21**

Every product has a purpose for which it was manufactured; likewise, man was formed by God for a purpose. God has clearly stated His intention for creating man, which is for His glory. From the 1st verse of Isaiah 43, God has rolled out several promises for His people in captivity. Without mincing words, He has declared to them, through the prophet, how He will deliver them from

Babylonian captivity and restore them back to their place of comfort and peace. And the reason for this is because of His glory.

Formed for Himself

"This shall be written for the generation to come: and the people which shall be created shall praise the LORD." - **Psalm 102:18**

God has formed the people for Himself, not for themselves, and the purpose is to preserve the remembrance of His name, to transmit the knowledge of the true God to future times, and to celebrate His praise. According to Calvin's commentary, "The Prophet means that the Lord will necessarily do what He formerly said because it concerns His glory to preserve the people whom He has chosen for Himself; and therefore, these words are intended for the consolation of the people."

The Scripture says in 2 Corinthians 5:15, "And that He died for all, that they which live should not henceforth live unto themselves, but unto Him which died for them, and rose again." This verse reveals that salvation is not a call to self but a call to live for Christ. Christ did not redeem you for you to do your will and fulfill your lust like before, but instead, you were saved and bought by His blood unto Him and transformed daily by His Word to conform to a new life in Christ.

Reflecting God's Praise

Therefore, our lives should show forth the praise of God. Peter said in 1 Peter 2:9, "But ye are a chosen generation, a royal priesthood, a holy nation, a peculiar people; that ye should show forth the praises of Him who hath called you out of darkness into His marvelous light." We are redeemed to show forth His praise, His glory, and His majesty.

God was about to set the people free from captivity and exile, and it will be by His mighty hand. So, it's time for Babylon and all other nations to know that there is a God in Israel. It's time to send a message to them, just like He told Pharaoh, that Israel is My Son, My first Son. It's time to robe the people with God's glory and restore them back to royalty.

That is what God is set to do in your life also. Whatever situation you may be going through presently, God is saying, for My glory's sake, I will come through for you. That should comfort you in your pain and give you the courage to trust God to the end.

Apostle Paul said in Ephesians 1:4-6, "According as He hath chosen us in Him before the foundation of the world, that we should be holy and without blame before Him in love: Having predestinated us unto the adoption of children by Jesus Christ to himself, according to the good pleasure of His will, to the praise of the glory of His grace, wherein He hath made us accepted in the beloved."

It goes to show you that the reason God places a premium on your life and the things that concern you is that none of His creation can show forth His praise like you. Isn't that amazing? God was saying, do you think that I will suffer My glory to fall to the ground? It is connected with your salvation, and therefore your salvation shall be the object of My care. In a word, know that you shall be saved because you cannot perish unless My glory likewise perishes. You shall, therefore, survive because I desire that you may continually proclaim My glory.

Zacharias said in Luke 1:74-75, "That he would grant unto us, that we being delivered out of the hand of our enemies might serve him without fear.

In holiness and righteousness before him, all the days of our life."

How do you show forth the Praise of God? By your deeds and works among men. Jesus said during His sermon in Matthew 5:14-16, "Ye are the light of the world. A city that is set on a hill cannot be hidden. Neither do men light a candle, and put it under a bushel, but on a candlestick; and it giveth light unto all that are in the house. Let your light so shine before men, that they may see your good works, and glorify your Father which is in Heaven." That is, the world is full of darkness, and you are redeemed to be the light for them to see. But that is only through your good works, first, from your house, among your family, and then to the world around.

Your lifestyle of love is the primary way to shine as light and show forth the praise of God on the Earth. They don't know Christ, and they are tired of people telling them about Christ; they desire to see Christ, and that can be possible through you. Show them the love of Christ, be an extension of truth and righteousness to the world around you. Be a reflection of the light of God to the dark world and a hope to the dying world. By so doing, men will glorify our Father in Heaven and be compelled to draw even closer to Him.

You see, the ultimate goal of our calling and consecration to God is so we may praise and honor Him forever. Therefore, as you journey up the hill, arm yourself with this truth, that you were not created for yourself, but for His glory. Let all your motives and intentions be to bring praise to His name; let your life draw the commendation of Heaven as a son and daughter in whom God is well pleased. Take away vain glory and self-seeking pursuit and seek the good for others with love.

And as you do, your life will be capsuled by a divine presence, which is evident with the cloud of glory.

ABOUT THE AUTHOR

Stephalyn Smith is a University graduate in the field of management. She is a Christian for over ten years and serves as a missionary and as a church secretary. She is a member of God of Mercy Tabernacle of Hope, Shepherd by Apostle Prophetess Pauline Mcknight Solomon, who assisted in her spiritual growth. She is a wife to the most supportive husband and mother of three beautiful children. Stephalyn is the firstborn in the union between her beautiful and supportive parents Sharon and Daniel Dunkley. She has four brothers and one sister.

THE JOURNEY UPHILL

www.ingramcontent.com/pod-product-compliance
Lightning Source LLC
Chambersburg PA
CBHW071542040426
42452CB00008B/1087